F.Y.I.

FASHION SOURCE

S0-CFX-207

NEW YORK CITY
2000

Editor in Chief, Co-Publisher
Tara Lowenberg

Managing Editor, Co-Publisher
Christopher Zalla

Senior Editor
Matthew Zalla

Editorial Consultants
Dale Burg
Elizabeth Schambelan

Research
Taylor Drotman
Andrew Grant
Caroline Grant
Danielle Lepiner
Terrence Lowenberg

Designed by Suzanne Kaloostian Adelhardt
with the help of Elaine Araujo.

© 1999 by F.Y.I. Fashion, Inc.

ISBN 1-930404-00-X

To Readers:
Neither F.Y.I. Fashion nor its contributors have any interest, financial or personal, in the locations listed in this book. No fees were paid or services rendered in exchange for inclusion in these pages.

Although every effort was made to ensure that all information was accurate and up-to-date at the time of publication, neither the publisher, nor its authors can be held responsible for any errors, omissions, or adverse consequences resulting from the use of such information. It is recommended that you call ahead to verify store information.

Consumers & retailers with questions and/or comments regarding any of F.Y.I. Fashion Source's guidebooks, products, and services may call 1-877-FYI-SHOP (1-877-394-7467) weekdays from 9AM to 5PM EST, or visit our website @ www.fyifashion.com.

Contents

Legend

TG 170
170 Ludlow St.   *(Houston/Stanton)*   *212-995-8660*

A Ludlow Street pioneer, TG 170 has shepherded several unknown designers into the major-leagues. Its concern for crediting lesser knowns is evident in its hip yet diverse selection. It still pays homage to those it discovered, and balances out its inventory with the trendy establishment. **Best Find: Karen Walker faux-fur neck warmer $178.**

· *Katayone Adeli Cords $136*

- **Albert Chan · Autumn Cashmere · Daryl K · Freitag**
- **Karen Walker · Katayone Adeli · Kooba · Laura Reilly**
- **Lauren Moffatt · Liz Collins · Patty Shelabarger · Paul & Joe**
- **Petit Bateau · Pixie Yates · Rebecca Dannenberg · Ripcosa**
- **Ruby Tuesday · Sally Penn · Samey Lula · Souchi · Terri Gillis**
- **TG 170 · The Wrights · Tooke · Ula Johnson · United Bamboo**

⊙ M-Sun 12-8
Store credit w/in 7 days w/ receipt

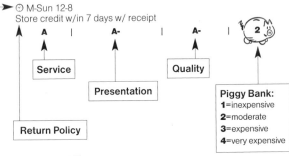

A | A | A- | A- | 2

F.Y.I. Fashion Source features over 500 of New York City's best women's clothing stores with over 1,500 labels. Each store entry contains the following store information:

Organization

This book is organized geographically by neighborhood, first by the avenues, then by the streets. Within each neighborhood, the avenues are ordered from west to east. Streets are organized from south to north above Houston, and from north to south below Houston.

Description

Provides a brief evaluation of the store including typical items carried, target customers, and/or noteworthy characteristics.

Best Find

Highlights outstanding items. While price is frequently taken into account when determining a best find, sometimes the item is so fabulous that price is not a consideration.

Sample Price

Allows readers to quickly size up pricing in a given store by specifying a particular item and its price.

Label List

A representative listing of the labels carried by individual stores. Some stores' label lists change frequently and others do not. While only thirty labels could be included with each store in the description portion of the book, a complete label inventory was included in the Label Locator. For example, if a store features over 400 labels, that store would appear under each of those labels in the Label Locator.

Store Hours

Store hours change frequently. Typically, stores open and close later in the summers, and have longer hours during peak shopping seasons. Many stores change their hours on a weekly basis and their listing is generalized for the year. Please call ahead to verify a store's hours.

Return Policy

Notes the type of policy (refund, store credit, or exchange) and time restrictions, if any, in which returns are allowable. Any special considerations/policies are also included.

Grading

All grades were awarded on a letter scale from A+ to F (with C considered to be average). F.Y.I. included only 500 of New York's best stores. Stores which received poor grades did not make the cut. The letter grades below each description correspond to their respective categories listed across the top of each page: Service, Presentation, and Quality.

Expense

Store expense levels are broken down into four categories and are represented by piggy banks.

To help you find specific labels and attractions, several indexes have been provided in the back of the book.

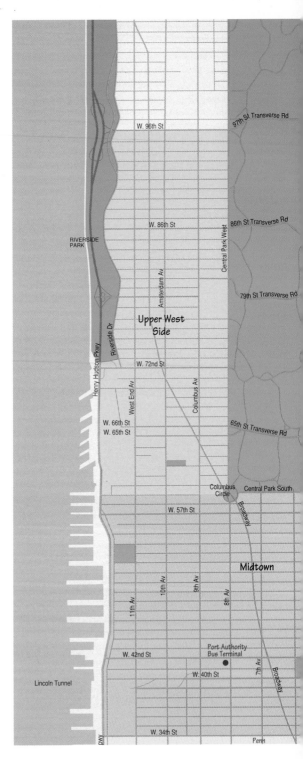

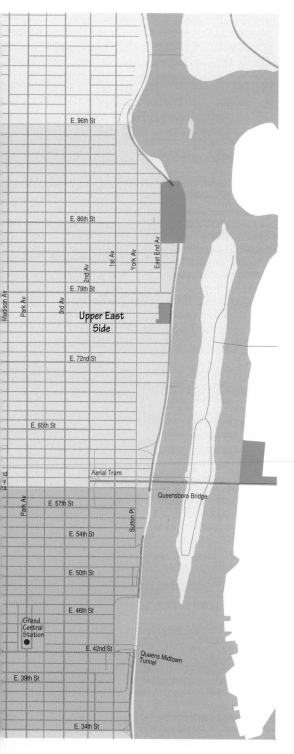

E. 96th St

E. 86th St

East End Av

1st Av

York Av

2nd Av

E. 79th St

Madison Av

Park Av

3rd Av

Upper East Side

E. 72nd St

E. 65th St

nd
y
a

Aerial Tram

Queensboro Bridge

Park Av

E. 57th St

Sutton Pl

E. 54th St

E. 50th St

E. 46th St

Grand
Central
Station

E. 42nd St

Queens Midtown
Tunnel

E. 39th St

E. 34th St

W. 34th St

Penn Station

Broadway

West Side Expwy

11th Av

Av of the Americas (6th Av)

5th Av

Madison Av

Chelsea

7th Av

W. 23rd St

W. 20th St

10th Av

9th Av

Flatiron District

W. 14th St

West Village

5th Av

University Pl

8th Av

Greenwich Av

W. 10th St

Greenwi

Waverly Pl

W. 8th St

Villa

W. 12th St

Greenwich St

W. 4th St

Bleecker St

Hudson St

Grove St

Perry St

Charles St

W. 10th St

Christopher St

7th Av

Waverly Pl

WASHINGTON SQUARE

Wa

Av of the Americas

Bleecker

W. Houston St

Sullivan St

SOHO

Pr

Thompson St

W. Broadway

Wooster St

Greene St

Mercer St

Sp

Hudson St

Canal St

St Clark

W. Broadway

Church St

Tribeca

Franklin St

Holland Tunnel

Dua

Reade St

West Side Expwy

Liberty St

Cortla

Broadway

HUDSON RIVER

Lower Manhattan

BAT
PA

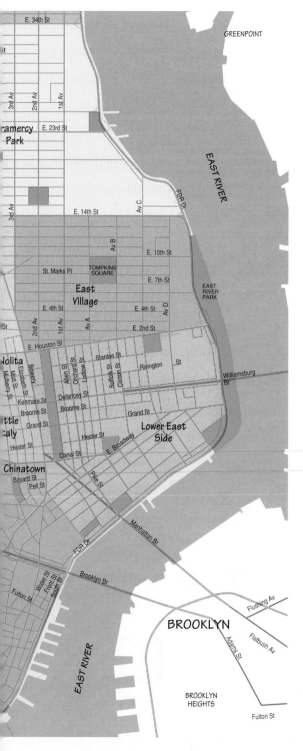

Upper
West Side

A Tempo
Ann Taylor*
Assets London
Banana Republic*
Barami*
Bati
Betsey Johnson*
Central Park West
Club Monaco*
Coach*
Diana & Jeffries*
Eileen Fisher*
Express*
French Connection*
Gap*
Kenneth Cole*
Liana
Lord of the Fleas*
Midali*
Montmartre*
New York Look*
Nine West*
Olive & Bette's*
Only Hearts
Patagonia
Really Great Things
Sacco
Tani
Tibet Bazaar
Tip Top Shoes
Varda*

*Additional locations can be found
in the Multiple Store Index pp. 152-159.

BROADWAY

Tani
2020 Broadway   *(69th/70th)*   212-873-4361

Making the most of a small space, Tani offers an extensive collection of hip shoes. Whether you want a flannel clog or a knee-high black leather boot, you're likely to find it here on the shelves overflowing with current styles. **Best Find: Haflinger wool clog style shoes $80.**

· *Knee-high boots $245*

· **BCBG** · **Berne Mev** · **Bettye Mueller** · **Charles David**
· **David Aaron** · **Haflinger** · **Naked Feet** · **Via Spiga**

🕐 M-F 10-8, Sat 10-7:30, Sun 12-7
Store credit w/in 14 days.

   C- | C | B+ | 2

Diana & Jeffries
2062 Broadway   *(70th/71st)*   212-874-2884

Diana & Jeffries showcases the hottest lines in town. Younger women who want up-to-the-minute mainstream fashion should definitely pencil this store into their shopping itineraries.

· *Knit mini by Nell $95*

· **614** · **ABS** · **Alice & Trixie** · **Bella Dahl** · **Bette Paige**
· **Big Star** · **Buzz 18** · **Catherine** · **Central Park West** · **Easel**
· **For Joseph** · **Iris Singer** · **Jane Doe** · **Jenne Maag**
· **Margaret O'Leary** · **Michael Stars** · **Nanette Lepore** · **Nell**
· **NKL** · **Shoshanna** · **Supply & Demand** · **Tease Tees** · **Theory**
· **Todd Oldham** · **Urchin** · **Vivienne Tam** · **White & Warren**

🕐 M-Sat 11-8, Sun 12-6
Store credit w/in 7 days w/ receipt.

   C | B- | A- | 3

Central Park West
2124 Broadway   *(74th/75th)*   212-579-3737

This store isn't big, but it's wall-to-wall with must-have items: the best pieces from the trendiest lines. Stop in and see why Central Park West is one of the most popular boutiques on the Upper West Side.

· *William B leopard skirt $198*

· **3 Dots** · **Ashley** · **Central Park West** · **Chaiken & Capone**
· **Earl Jeans** · **F.r.e.e.** · **FGL** · **IS** · **JET** · **Katayone Adeli**
· **Levi's** · **Michael Stars** · **Tank** · **Tease Tees** · **Trina Turk**
· **William B**

🕐 M-Th 11-10, F 11-7:30, Sat 11-7, Sun 12-6
Store w/ receipt.

   A | B+ | A- | 3

Lord of the Fleas
2142 Broadway   *(75th/76th)*   212-875-8815

For a cheap thrill, dress yourself up for a night or two on the town in an outfit from Lord of the Fleas. The funky styles and cheap stretch fabrics won't outlast any trend, but the young and fickle who want to reinvent themselves overnight shouldn't mind.

· *T-shirts with kitschy prints $22*

· **Bulldog** · **Flyby** · **Free People** · **Hourglass** · **Illig** · **Kangol**
· **Lord of the Fleas** · **Lord of the Fleas** · **Z. Cavaricci** · **Zoom**

🕐 M-Sun 11-8:30
Store credit w/in 7 days w/ receipt.

   C+ | C- | C+ | 2

UPPER WEST SIDE

Montmartre
2212 Broadway   (78th/79th)   212-875-8430

Everything in this wanna-be Parisian boutique is stuff you've seen before—but it looks exciting all together in one room. It has the same popular fare as its sister store on Broadway with skinny pants and fitted sweaters that, though youthful, are not only for the young.

· *Rebecca Taylor mohair sweater $202*

· **BCBG** · **Bianca Nero** · **Chaiken & Capone** · **Custo**
· **Diane Von Furstenberg** · **Katayone Adeli** · **Rebecca Taylor**

☺ M-Sat 11-8, Sun 12-7
Store credit w/in 10 days.

| C+ | | B | | B- | | |

Bati
2323 Broadway   (84th/85th)   212-724-7214

A little piece of Soho on upper Broadway, Bati carries a number of European shoe lines, including BCBG, Moschino, and its own house line. If you want the most current popular styles, Bati will be up your alley.

· *Prada inspired boots with suede and patent leather $148*

· **Bati** · **BCBG** · **Gianni Bravo** · **L'Autre Chose** · **Le Tini**
· **Luca Del Monde** · **Miss Rossi** · **Moda Italia** · **Moschino**

☺ M-Sat 11-8, Sun 12-7
Store credit w/in 7 days w/ receipt.

| C+ | | B | | B | | |

Tibet Bazaar
473 Amsterdam Ave.   (82nd/83rd)   212-595-8487

Open the door to this pretty boutique and your senses will be happily overwhelmed, thanks to the odor of incense wafting through the shop and the bright splashes of color hanging on the walls. Beautiful crinkly tie-dye scarves are a cool alternative to the ever-ubiquitous pashmina, and the exotic pillow-cases and bed-spreads are a phenomenal way to liven up a drab bedroom. **Best Find: Silk and cotton tie-dyed scarves $75.**

· *Pashminas $250*

· **N/A**

☺ M-Sun 11-7
Store credit w/in 7 days w/ receipt.

| B+ | | B+ | | B+ | | |

Betsey Johnson
248 Columbus Ave.   (71st/72nd)   212-362-3364

In the 1960s, Betsey Johnson's avant-garde psychedelic dresses made her a favorite of Andy Warhol's crowd, and ever since—even through the dark days of mid-90s minimalism—Johnson has continued to produce colorful designs that combine glamour with a spark of eccentricity. **Best Find: Small leopard bag $66.**

· *Ankle-length dress $240*

· **Betsey Johnson**

☺ M-Sat 11-7, Sun 12-7
Store credit w/in 14 days.

| A- | | B+ | | A- | | |

COLUMBUS AVENUE

Olive & Bette's
252 Columbus Ave.   (71st/72nd)   *212-579-2178*

Young and fun, or at least young at heart, Olive & Bette's has something for everybody. It carries the same merchandise as its East Side counterpart—from kitschy shirts to snug-fitting pants.

· *Cotton skirt $250*

· **Bette Paige** · **Bisou Bisou** · **Claudine Penedo** · **Daryl K**
· **Diab'less** · **Diane Von Furstenberg** · **Diesel** · **Earl Jeans**
· **Easel** · **Free People** · **JET** · **Jill Stuart** · **Juicy Couture**
· **Katayone Adeli** · **Le Havlin Piro** · **Michael Stars** · **Miguelena**
· **Olive & Bette** · **Petro Zillia** · **Shoshanna** · **Susanna Monaco**
· **Theory** · **Vivienne Tam** · **William B**

☺ M-Sat 11-8, Sun 11-7
Store credit w/in 10 days w/ receipt.

   A- | **B+** | **A-** | 3

Really Great Things
284 Columbus Ave.   (73rd/74th)   *212-787-5354*

More accurately, this should be called Somewhat Nice Things. It's an odd mix of signature pieces, like a long bouclé coat or snake-skin bag, along with several lines by unknown European designers.

· *Sara Sturgeon long wool coat $1150*

· **Gucci** · **Le Monde Du Baggage** · **Petro Zillia** · **Sara Sturgeon**

☺ M-Sat 12-7, Sun 1-6
Store credit w/in 7 days w/ receipt.

   B- | **B** | **A-** | 3

A Tempo
290 Columbus Ave.   (73rd/74th)   *212-769-0368*

A Tempo is an excellent destination for high school seniors who have left prom dress shopping to the last minute. There are lots of choices on the overflowing racks, but you'll have to spend some time hunting for the cream of the crop.

· *Sparkling net shawls $149*

· **ABS** · **Collections** · **Knots** · **Laundry** · **Sue Wong** · **Tessuto**
· **Weston Wear** · **Yigal Aʐrouel**

☺ M-Sat 11-8, Sun 12-7
Store credit w/in 7 days.

   C+ | **C-** | **B-** | 2

Liana
324 Columbus Ave.   (75th/76th)   *212-873-8746*

For those weddings and other functions you don't want to go to, Liana can at least dress you stylishly, affordably and painlessly. The crêpe cocktail dresses and satin evening gowns are great for proms or other youthful formal functions. The store features trendy daywear too.

· *Formal dress $300*

· **3 Dots** · **Alex Garfield** · **Andrew Marc** · **Bianca Nero**
· **Diane Von Furstenberg** · **Laundry** · **Mandalay**
· **Nanette Lepore** · **Nicole Miller** · **Supply & Demand**
· **Tahari** · **Theory** · **Vivienne Tam**

☺ M-Sat 11-7, Sun 1-6
Store credit w/in 7 days.
Sale items and evening wear final.

   B+ | **B+** | **A-** | 3

Midali
330 Columbus Ave. (75th/76th) 212-873-5451

Mature women who want to wear contemporary fashion instead of frumpy frocks can find an interesting mix of clothes at Midali. The cuts are on the conservative side but the clothes have a bit of European flair, and the colors and patterns give them real personality.

· *Wool suit $400*

· **Martino Midali**

☺ T-Sat 11-7, Sun 12-6
Store credit w/in 7 days.

B+ | B+ | A- | 3

Only Hearts
386 Columbus Ave. (78th/79th) 212-724-5608

This Columbus Avenue war horse has been selling a great combination of sweet and sexy lingerie for years and is a great source for adorable bridal shower gifts. Brightly colored lace tanks can double up as evening wear, and for a night at home you can find both comfy nightgowns and vixen-ish slips. **Best Find: Only Hearts gauze double layer skirt $78.**

· *Bra and underwear set $40*

· **Andrés · Christine · Felina · Gemma · Lounge Act**
· **Mes Dessous · Nick & Nora · NK · Only Hearts · Parisa**

☺ M-Sat 11-8, Sun 12-6
Store credit w/in 7 days.

C+ | B | B+ | 2

Patagonia
426 Columbus Ave. (80th/81st) 917-441-0011

Nothing is as soft, warm, and useful as a fleece from Patagonia. There isn't much else to buy in the camping-geared store, but everyone should have a cozy fleece pullover or jacket.

· *R3 zippered fleece $134*

· **Patagonia**

☺ M-Sat 11-8, Sun 12-7
Refund w/ tags & receipt.

B- | C+ | A- | 3

Assets London
464 Columbus Ave. (82nd/83rd) 212-874-8253

This British boutique carries a great selection of international lines that would be fashionable on any continent. Wool pants in pretty pastels with matching coats, as well as handbags, trendy shoes, and sexy dresses fill the racks. The current styles are translated into different fabrics and colors for an endless selection of fun clothes.

· *Wool pants $295*

· **Anna Sui · Antik Batik · Barbara Bui · Birkenstock**
· **Chaiken & Capone · D&G · Duffy · E-play · Farrutx · Gym**
· **Jussara · Kangol · Kayzo · Kostum · Les Prairies de Paris**
· **Mane-Sho · Miki Mialy · Paul & Joe · Plein Sud**
· **Rue Blanche · Zydeco**

☺ M-Sat 11-8, Sun 12-7
Store credit w/in 7 days w/ receipt. Sale items final.

A | A- | A- | 3

service | presentation | quality | expense

Tip Top Shoes
155 West 72nd St. (Broadway/Columbus) 212-787-4960

Don't be fooled by Tip-Top's appearance: it is not an old lady's shoe store. It is simply a very uncool space with some very hip shoes. Fashionistas seeking Birkenstocks in every variety, from flannel to pony-hair, should not miss the complete selection. Don't look here to find out what will be in W next month, but do come in if you're after a good selection of comfortable daytime shoes.

· *Pony Birkenstocks $130*

- **· Aerosoles · Aquatalia · BCBG · Beauty Feel · Birkenstock**
- **· Clark's · David Aaron · Donald Pliner · Ecco · Haflinger**
- **· Mephisto · Paul Green · Peter Kaiser · Rockport**
- **· Steve Madden · Stuart Weitzman · Timberland**

☉ M-Sat 9:30-6:45, Th 9:30-7:45, Sun 12-5
Refund w/in 5 days if unworn.
Exchange w/in 10 days.

C+ | B+ | B+ |

Upper East Side

Agnès B. *
Alicia Mugetti
Ann Taylor*
Ann Taylor Loft*
Anik*
Artbag
Ashanti
Banana Republic*
Barami*
Barneys New Yprk
BCBG Max Azria
Bebe*
Berk
Betsey Bunky Nini
Betsey Johnson*
Big Drop*
Billy Martin's
Bis
Bloomingdale's
Bottega Venetta
Bra Smyth
Calvin Klein
Calypso St. Barth*
Cashmere Cashmere
Cashmere NY
Cerruti
Charles Jourdan
Chlöe
Christian Louboutin
Chuckies*
Cinco
Club Monaco*
Coach*
Danielle B.
Delle Celle
Diana & Jeffries
Diesel
DKNY
Dolce & Gabbana
Eileen Fisher*
Emanuel Ungaro
Emilio Pucci
En Soie
Encore

Equipment
Express*
Fogal*
Fopp's*
Forreal Basics*
Franceska
French Sole
Furla
Gamine
Gap*
Gianfranco Ferre
Giorgio Armani
Iceberg
Intermix*
Issey Miyake
Jennifer Tyler*
Jimmy's
Joan & David*
Joseph
Joseph (pant store)*
Kenzo
Krizia
La Boutique Resale
La Perla
Lee Anderson
Leggiadro
Les Copains
Loro Piana
Luca Luca*
Malo
Manrico
Maraolo*
Marina Rinaldi
Martier
Martinez Valero
Max Mara
Ménage à Trois
Michael's
Midali*
Missoni
Mom's Night Out/
One Night Out
Morgane Le Fay*
Nara

Nicole Miller*
Nine West*
Nocturne
Oilily
Olive & Bette's*
Patrick Cox
Pelle Via Roma
Polo Sport*
Portantina
Prada
Precision*
Ralph Lauren
Rapax
René Collections
Robert Clergerie
Roberto Cavalli
Rose Marie Roussel
San Francisco
Clothing Co.
Scoop*
Searle*
Sergio Rossi
Shanghai Tang
Sonia Rykiel
Stephane Kelian
Steven Stolman
Sylvia Pine's
Uniquities
The Original
Leather Store*
Timberland
Tod's
TSE Cashmere
Urban Outfitters*
Unisa
Varda*
Vera Wang
Versace
Vertigo
Via Spiga
Victoria's Secret*
Vincent & Edgar
Vivaldi
Yves Saint Laurent

*Additional locations can be found
in the Multiple Store Index pp. 152-159.

MADISON AVENUE

Bottega Veneta
635 Madison Ave.   *(59th/60th)*   212-371-5511

It is a mystery why this label doesn't have the cachet of Prada and Fendi. Perhaps the answer is that it's a little less current and a lot more timeless, which doesn't appeal to the heat-of-the-moment fashion crowd. Still, Bottega designs a fabulous line of clothing in sumptuous fabrics and has an unbelievable selection of bags.

· *Leopard and pink silk reversible bag $500*

· **Bottega Veneta**

🕐 M-Sat 10-6, Th 10-7
Refund w/in 10 days w/ receipt.

    A- | **A-** | **A+** | 4

Tod's
650 Madison Ave.   *(59th/60th)*   212-644-5954

Of course every wardrobe could use a Tod's bag and a pair of driving shoes; unfortunately, not everyone can afford them. But if you win the lottery, head directly here to get several pairs of shoes with a bag to match. Tod's merchandise is classic yet eternally modern, and it comes in many different looks, from red patent leather to classic brown alligator.

· *Leather driving moccasins $295*

· **Tod's**

🕐 M-Sat 10-6, Sun 12-5
Store credit w/in 10 days.
Refund for phone orders w/in 10 days.

    B- | **B+** | **A+** | 4

Calvin Klein
654 Madison Ave.   *(@ 60th)*   212-292-9000

If minimalism isn't your thing, this stark store may convert you. Or not. But most people find Klein's beautiful, modern, pared-down clothing quite compelling. Colors are neutral and cuts are simple, but somehow the designs always look fresh.

· *Strappy high-heels $300*

· **Calvin Klein**

🕐 M-Sat 10-6, Th 10-8, Sun 12-6
Refund w/in 10 days. Store credit afterward.

    C+ | **A** | **A+** | 4

DKNY
655 Madison Ave.   *(@ 60th)*   212-223-3569

Donna seems to have lost her way when she left black matte jersey behind. Now, she's all about blinding primary colors on everything from bags to coats, which all share space in this impressive shop.

· *Super-thick wool sweater (with funnel-neck) $325*

· **DKNY**

🕐 M-Sat 10-7, Th 10-9, Sun 12-6
Refund w/in 10 days w/ receipt.
Store credit w/in 30 days.

    C+ | **A** | **A-** | 3

service | presentation | quality | expense

Barneys New York
660 Madison Ave.   *(60th/61st)*   212-826-8900

Spread out over Barneys' seven floors, you will find New York's most ambitious assortment of uncommon, fashion-forward clothing and accessories. The cool, laid-back atmosphere makes the shopping experience a pleasurable one, although the sales staff is at best aloof (unless you appear to be worth millions). The Co-op on the seventh floor feels more downtown than downtown, featuring a wide range of edgy, less expensive items from both obscure and popular designers. **Best Find: Hervé Chepalier bag $85.**

· *Wool sweater $178*

Labels include: Angel Sanchez · Antik Batik · Azzedine Alaïa · Barneys New York · Capucine Puerari · Chlöe · Christopher Totman · Colette Dinnegan · Elspeth Gibson · Helmut Lang · Hussein Chalayan · Jill Stuart · Lauren Moffatt · Les Prairies de Paris · Lucien Pellat-Finet · Marc Jacobs · Martin Margiela · Matthew Williamson · Milk Fed · Miu Miu · Paul Smith · Phillip Chi · Prada · Rebecca Dannenberg · Thimister · Tufi Duek · Uni Form · Vera Wang · William B · Wynn Wink · Yigal Azrouel · Yohji Yamamoto · Jean Yu · Zero

☺ M-F 10-8, Sat 10-7, Sun 12-6
Refund w/in 30 days w/ receipt.
Store credit w/outut receipt.

D+ | A+ | A+ |

Fogal
680 Madison Ave.   *(61st/62nd)*   212-759-9782

Over 80 colors and a variety of patterns of stockings are jammed into this compact Swiss hosiery boutique. If you're already up to your ears in stockings, check out the selection of bodysuits, swimwear and lingerie also offered at Fogal. Prices are a bit steep for hosiery, but you're paying for high quality.

· *Cashmere tights $350*

· **Fogal**

☺ M-Sat 10-6:30, Th 10-8
Refund if unopened w/ receipt.

A- | B | A+ |

Robert Clergerie
681 Madison Ave.   *(61st/62nd)*   212-207-8600

For sturdy shoes with style, check out Robert Clergerie. He designs modern updates of classic favorites, like loafers and chic boots, in tasteful but unexpected colors that are just enough to give an outfit that extra oomph.

· *Gregor loafers $360*

· **Robert Clergerie**

☺ M-F 10-6:30, Sat 10-6
Refund w/in 10 days w/ receipt.
Store credit afterwards.

B- | B+ | A |

MADISON AVENUE

Luca Luca
690 Madison Ave. (@ 62nd) 212-755-2444

Though catering to a mature, wealthier clientele, Luca Luca offers several items for the hipper, younger Manhattanite: fitted wool coats styled a la Audrey Hepburn in the winter, and beautiful, flowing chiffon blouses and evening gowns in the summer. This dramatic space compliments the high styles.

· *Pané velvet dress, $1800*

· **Luca Luca**

☺ M-Sat 10-6:30, Th 10-8
Store credit w/ receipt.

B-	A	A+	

Nocturne
698 Madison Ave. (62nd/63rd) 212-750-2951

This sleepytime boutique carries delicate nightgowns, cozy pajamas, and beautiful white cotton-and-lace nightgowns in mother and daughter sizes. This is a great place to find a sweet and unusual gift. It's also a terrific source for exquisite, old-fashioned christening gowns.

· *Mother/daughter nightgowns, $160/$110*

· **Canyon Group · Nautica · Nick & Nora · Nocturne**
· **Priamo · Vera Bradley · Verena**

☺ M-Sat 10-7, Sun 12-5
Store credit w/ receipt.

B	B	A-	

Rose Marie Roussel
700 Madison Ave., 2nd Floor (62nd/63rd) 212-421-8677

For eighteen years, savvy customers have been heading up the flight of stairs that leads to this custom dress shop. Ms. Rousell's creations are the choice of the forty-plus crowd that includes Bar and Bat Mitzvah moms, mothers of the bride, and any woman with a frequent need to gown up. Though the styles aren't the last word, you get high quality here, from craftsmanship to materials.

· *Evening dress $2500*

· **Rose Marie Roussel**

☺ M-F 11-6, Sat by appt. only
Store credit w/in 8 days.

B+	B-	A	

Leggiadro
700 Madison Ave. (62nd/63rd) 212-753-5050

Be sure to seek out this hard-to-spot Madison Avenue boutique. An amazingly colorful selection of imported cashmere cable knits, oxford blouses, and exquisite scarves awaits. The Jack Rogers flip-flops are adorable and ideal for every summer outfit. **Best Find: Colorful cashmere scarf $325**.

· *Cable-knit cashmere sweater $650*

· **Cashmere Studio · Clara Cottmann · Craig Taylor · Drumohr**
· **Gunext · Incotex · Jack Rogers · Kiss My Feet · Leggiadro**
· **Lorenzini · Sugar**

☺ M-Sat 10:30-6
Store credit w/in 7 days. Swimwear and sale items final.

B+	B+	A	

Unisa
701 Madison Ave.   (62nd/63rd)   212-753-7474

Consider yourselves warned: The selection of designer styles at very, very friendly prices makes it virtually impossible to leave Unisa empty-handed. When you find yourself in need of a strappy bubblegum-pink patent-leather stiletto that from a distance could be mistaken for a Manolo, stop in. And while you're here, pick up a pair of simple ballet flats.

· *Prada mule knock-offs $98*

· **Unisa**

☉ M-Sat 10-6:30, Sun 12-5
Store credit or exchange w/in 14 days.
Sale items final.

B+		B+		B+		2

Patrick Cox
702 Madison Ave.   (62nd/63rd)   212-759-3910

This downtown-style shoe store seems a bit out of place on Madison Avenue but is a good place to locate a chic treat for your feet. The store is filled with colorful shoes in odd styles that will cure anyone suffering from the black-shoe doldrums.

· *Orange mules $356*

· **Patrick Cox**

☉ M-Sat 11-7, Sun 12-5
Store credit w/in 14 days w/ receipt.

C+		B		A-		3

Timberland
709 Madison Ave.   (62nd/63rd)   212-754-0434

In the middle of Madison Avenue, a wilderness oasis. An unpretentious specialty store geared to lovers of the outdoors, Timberland is the pinnacle of granola chic and the place to go for cool hiking boots. Stop in, have a swig of carrot juice, and get in touch with your earthy side.

· *Hiking boots $80*

· **Timberland**

☉ M-F 9:30-7, Sat-Sun 10-6
Refund w/in 60 days w/ receipt.
Current price w/out.

B+		B+		A-		2

Roberto Cavalli
711 Madison Ave.   (@ 63rd)   212-755-7722

Imagine a merger of Gucci and Versace and you'd get Cavalli. The aesthetic is maximalist: everything is ruffled, bedazzled, sequined, or embroidered, not to mention outrageously colored with clashing prints. The stylish clothes are very Italian, and even the sales staff is sassy in this wild and crazy shop.

· *Sequined or hand-painted stretch jeans $490-$680*

· **Roberto Cavalli**

☉ M-Sat 10-6
Store credit w/in 7 days.

C		A		A		4

MADISON AVENUE

Shanghai Tang
714 Madison Ave.   (@ 63rd)   **212-888-5262**

This store has built an extensive collection on modern reproductions of the Chinese pajama. Beautiful sweaters, tunic-style T-shirts, and pajama-style suits in exquisite fabrics make excellent additions to any wardrobe. The casual line is priced very reasonably, but if you really want to splurge, have a custom piece made.

· *Silk Chinese pajama $245*
· **Shanghai Tang**
☺ M-Sat 10-7, Sun 12-6
Store credit w/in 30 days w/ receipt.

B | **A-** | **A-** | (3)

Stephane Kélian
717 Madison Ave.   (63rd/64th)   **212-980-1919**

An Upper East Side favorite for shoes, Stephane Kélian offers women a diversion from boring flats. Every shoe you'll find here has its own distinctive look, whether it's a gold woven platform, open-toed mule, or simple black ankle boot with a wedge heel.

· *Microfiber ankle-length boots $350*
· **Stephane Kélian**
☺ M-Sat 10-6
Store credit w/in 10 days w/ receipt.

C+ | **B** | **A** | (3)

Furla
727 Madison Ave.   (63rd/64th)   **212-755-8986**

A reasonably-priced bag store that gives good style and good leather for the money. A perfect destination for career women who want a functional work bag that doubles as a chic fashion accessory.

· *Classic leather bag $145*
· **Furla**
☺ M-F 10-6, Sat 12-6
Exchange or store credit w/in
2-3 wks if merchandise unused.

C+ | **A** | **A** | (3)

Artbag
735 Madison Ave.   (@ 64th)   **212-744-2720**

If you can't afford the real thing, this is the place for the next best. Though Artbag will never admit it, the shop carries fantastic copies of all of the Hermès, Tod's and Gucci bags. If it doesn't come in a color you like, Artbag will customize to suit your tastes. The store can also refurbish an old bag in need.

· *Birken bag $600*
· **Artbag**
☺ M-Fri 9:30-5:45, Sat 10-5
Store credit.

C+ | **C-** | **A** | (3)

BCBG Max Azria
744 Madison Ave.   *(64th/65th)*   *212-794-7124*

Like the main store, this branch gives a lot of bang for your buck. The clothes are elegant, but very up-to-the-moment and fairly priced. Women of all ages will appreciate the high quality and classic styles this boutique offers. **Best Find: Ankle-length shearling coat $1038.**

· *Wool and silk turtleneck sweater $258*
· **BCBG**

⏱ M-Sat 11-7, Th 11-8, Sun 12-6
Store credit w/in 10 days w/ receipt.

A | **A-** | **A-** |

Morgane Le Fay
746 Madison Ave.   *(64th/65th)*   *212-879-9700*

Layering is big here; so are drab colors. The clothes emphasize the waist in a Romantic, Victorian way, which may not be flattering to your body. If you can sift through the strange pieces and make yourself try them on, you may be pleasantly surprised by the merchandise, which is guaranteed to add a touch of fantasy to your wardrobe. **Best Find: Red velvet gown $1600.**

· *Light wool ankle-length skirt with satin trim at waist $340*
· **Morgane Le Fay**

⏱ M-Sat 10-6
Store credit w/in 7 days.

C- | **B** | **A** |

Giorgio Armani
760 Madison Ave.   *(@ 65th)*   *212-988-9191*

Armani is one of the greats. His classic styles and exquisite cuts have made him a favorite of women across all fashion boundaries. From simple suits which fit as though they were custom-tailored to drop-dead beaded evening gowns, Armani's designs shine at making women look sexy, but not trashy. Unfortunately, only the privileged few can afford the fruit of his talents.

· *Beaded evening gowns beginning at $10,000*
· **Giorgio Armani**

⏱ M-Sat 10-6, Th 10-7
Return to method of payment w/in
10 days w/ receipt.

B+ | **A+** | **A+** | (4)

Vertigo
755 Madison Ave.   *(65th/66th)*   *212-439-9626*

If you are slender and like to flaunt it, Vertigo makes great pants that will show off a long, skinny leg. The house line is an excellent source of work clothes for women who have to wear suits but still want style. The very fitted jackets are just as flattering as the stylish pants.

· *Vertigo suit, $500*
· **Vertigo**

⏱ M-Sat 10-7, Th 10-8, Sun 12-6
Store credit w/in 7 days.

B- | **B** | **A-** |

MADISON AVENUE

Via Spiga
765 Madison Ave.   (65th/66th)   212-988-4877

Possibly the best place in town to get a deal on shoes. The selection here is always stylish and reasonably priced, and best of all, generally comfortable. Classics like loafers are made over in new colors, while Prada-esque wedge sandals and flip-flops pay homage to youthful trends.

· *High-heeled Mary Janes $160*

· **Via Spiga**

☺ M-Sat 10-6, Sun 12-5
Refund w/in 7 days w/ receipt.
Store credit w/in 14 days.

| B+ | B+ | A- | 2 |

Krizia
769 Madison Ave.   (@ 66th)   212-879-1211

The misleading windows suggest that edgy clothing awaits inside, but customers will find that the asymmetric hemlines and necklines are balanced with straightforward suits. The exceptional quality knit sweater dresses, skirts, and wide, thick scarves are real luxury investments. **Best Find: Extra-long and thick wool scarf $210.**

· *Wool suits $1100-$2200*

· **Krizia**

☺ M-F 10-6, Th 10-7:30, Sat 10-6
Store credit w/in 7 days.

| B- | B+ | A | 4 |

BCBG Max Azria
770 Madison Ave.   (@ 66th)   212-717-4225

The good news is that this is one of the best collections of mid-level designers in the fashion industry, a place where you'll never obsess over one item because the whole collection is spectacular. The clothes are always modernized to suit the times yet classic in their cuts and styles. The bad news is that the rude sales people detract from the pleasure of the shopping experience.

· *Chunky red sleeveless turtleneck $245*

· **BCBG**

☺ M-Sat 10-7, Th 10-8, Sun 12-6
Store credit.

| D+ | A- | A- | 3 |

Iceberg
772 Madison Ave.   (@ 66th)   212-249-5412

This Madison Avenue cool spot is a mixed bag. Some clothes, like cashmere sweaters with patchwork prints and sequins, have a playful feel, while others, such as plain shifts, are more reserved. The eclectic blend of styles will appeal most to the young, whimsical, and well-off.

· *Patchwork wool sequined sweater $525*

· **Iceberg**

☺ M-Sat 10-6, Th 10-7
Store credit.

| B+ | B+ | A | 4 |

La Perla
777 Madison Ave. (66th/67th) 212-570-0050

An exquisite line of lingerie for the self-indulgent. Customers can find white eyelet or orange lace bras with matching panties to tempt a new lover or reinvigorate an old one. Always elegant but never stuffy, La Perla also carries slinky, sexy (but not trashy) evening dresses for those buff enough to wear items that caress every curve. **Best Find: Evening dress $1000**.

· *Off-white lace bra $185*

· **La Perla**

☺ M-Sat 10-6
Store credit or exchange w/in 10 days w/ receipt.

C+ | B+ | A |

Charles Jourdan
777 Madison Ave. (66th/67th) 212-585-2238

Once a pre-eminent name in shoes, Jourdan has lost some status but seems more accessible and much cooler these days. The designs are cutting-edge chic and appeal to a much younger crowd, who snap up the classic flats and snakeskin mules with geometric platforms at reasonable prices.

· *Snakeskin print geometric heel sandal $175*

· **Charles Jourdan**

☺ M-Sun 10-7
Refund w/in 10 days w/ receipt.
Handbags, accessories, and sale items final.

C- | B- | B+ |

Nicole Miller
780 Madison Ave. (66th/67th) 212-288-9779

Nicole Miller has built her empire on the kitschy patterns and classic styles which define her line of elegant evening attire. Though the prints sometimes get a little too crazy, Nicole Miller remains a great resource for dress wear.

· *Satin column dress $250*

· **Nicole Miller**

☺ M-F 10-7, Sat 10-6
Store credit w/in 7 days w/ receipt.
Evening wear sales final.

C+ | A- | A- |

Berk
781 Madison Ave. (66th/67th) 212-570-0285

This stuffy shop, a Madison Avenue staple, carries a fine collection of conservative cashmere goods. The styles and prices attract the "ladies who lunch" crowd, whom the sales people seem to prefer. If you're young and hip, chances are you'll be ignored until you show them the money.

· *Cashmere scarf $195*

· **Berk Cashmere**

☺ M-Sat 10-6
Store credit or exchange w/in
30 days w/ tags and receipt.

C | B- | A |

MADISON AVENUE

Varda
786 Madison Ave.   (66th/67th)   212-472-7552

Varda serves the footwear needs of uptown professionals who yearn for downtown style. The loafers and boots are timeless and understated, while also embodying the cool minimalism that prevails south of Houston Street. You'll also find the occasional sandal that suits for casual Fridays.

· *Riding boots $350*
· **Varda**
☺ M-Sat 10-7
Store credit w/in 7 days w/ receipt.

| B- | B | A | |

Cerruti
789 Madison Ave.   (66th/67th)   212-327-2222

This multi-floor fashion house has abandoned its former stuffy ways. From a simply cut pant to a fur vest, Cerruti dresses the financial elite in super-stylish ensembles.

· *Pony gloves with leather $495*
· **Cerruti 1881 · Cerruti Arte**
☺ M-Sat 10-6, Th 10-7
Store credit w/in 10 days.

| A- | A- | A | |

Emanuel Ungaro
792 Madison Ave.   (@ 67th)   212-249-4090

Ungaro wins the prize for The Store Most In Need of a Make-over. The 80s ambience might overwhelm a lesser designer's clothing. However, Ungaro's sexy, feminine, floral dresses—some ornamented with beads and ruffles, others cut to reveal your curves—are ideal for women who enjoy playing dress-up.

· *Pink silk, lace, and beaded slip dress $5000*
· **Emanuel Ungaro**
☺ M-Sat 10-6
Store credit w/in 10 days.

| C | B+ | A+ | |

Joseph
796 Madison Ave.   (67th/68th)   212-327-1773

Joseph has chic, stylish clothing down to a science. Luxurious materials are transformed into classic yet sexy skirts, thick chunky sweaters, flowing little dresses, and fabulous form-fitting shearling coats. Though the sales help is notoriously nasty and the prices are high, few stores can compete with this line. **Best Find: Red velour stretch pants $299.**

· *Thick cashmere turtleneck $600*
· **Joseph**
☺ M-Sat 10-6:30, Th 10-7, Sun 1-6
Store credit w/in 14 days.

| D | B | A | |

Ménage à Trois
799 Madison Ave., 2nd Floor (67th/68th) 212-396-2514

Don't let one flight of stairs deter you from checking out this fabulous collection. Ménage à Trois proves that some of Madison Avenue's greatest treasures are hidden one flight above ground level. Most of the clothes are designed for evening wear and range from taffeta mermaid skirts to leather bustiers and matching pants. Alongside Downtown offbeat-cool styles are designs that reflect classic Uptown sensibility. **Best Find: Hand-painted corset in duchess satin $850.**

· *Taffeta and satin mermaid skirt $875*

· **Ménage à Trois**

⊙ M-F 8:30-6, Sat 10-5
Store credit w/in 14 days.

A+ | A- | A- |

Marina Rinaldi
800 Madison Ave. (67th/68th) 212-734-4333

A division of Max Mara, Marina Rinaldi is a plus-size store with serious style. Rinaldi realizes some women are bigger than size 6 and picks up where the rest have left off, so suede wrap skirts and formal evening gowns are as current and fabulous as the clothes in all the other stores on Madison Avenue. It makes one wonder why no one else takes the time to make larger sizes fashionable.

· *Suede wrap skirt $1040*

· **Marina Rinaldi**

⊙ M-Sat 10-6, W-Th 10-7
Store credit w/in 5 days.

A- | A- | A |

Manrico
802 Madison Ave. (67th/68th) 212-794-4200

This store carries a sumptuous collection of ultra-fine-quality cashmere sweaters in a rainbow of hues. The pieces are available in classic, roomy shapes as well as newer, more delicate body-conscious styles. Manrico also carries voluminous scarves and warm coats for bitter cold winter days.

· *Twin set: shell $350, Cardigan $450*

· **Manrico**

⊙ M-Sat 10-6, Sun 12-5
Store credit w/in 10 days.

B+ | A- | A |

Joseph (pant store)
804 Madison Ave. (67th/68th) 212-570-0077

The demand for these sexy, slender pants was so great that Joseph had to open a store dedicated to the fashion favorite. This small store houses an infinite supply of the chicest pants in town. Alas: if you haven't got the legs of a fashion model, you may have trouble sliding them on.

· *Tuxedo-style pants $245*

· **Joseph**

⊙ M-Sat 10-6:30, Th 10-7, Sun 1-6
Exchange w/in 5 days.

C | B | A- |

UPPER EAST SIDE

MADISON AVENUE

Kenzo
805 Madison Ave.   *(67th/68th)*   *212-717-0101*

Eye-catching windows will lure you into this expensive boutique, and the colorful knits will make you linger. Kenzo appeals to an older crowd, with generous cuts and muted colors. The occasional jacket translates from day to evening wear, and the wool scarves will give a solid color coat a real boost.

· *Mohair/wool embroidered scarves $350*

· **Kenzo**

☺ M-Sat 10-6, Th 10-7
Store credit w/in 5 days.

C+ | A- | A |

Les Copains
807 Madison Ave.   *(67th/68th)*   *212-327-3014*

The cream-colored boutique softly exhorts a sophisticated client to indulge herself. The lavish sweaters with fur trim and matching knee length skirts and pants are super-soft. However, the vast space leaves the predatory sales help with little to do but follow you around, sullying the blissful experience.

· *Cashmere wool lycra sweater with mink trim $575*

· **Les Copains**

☺ M-Sat 10-6, Th 10-7
Store credit w/in 10 days.

C- | A | A |

Billy Martin's
810 Madison Ave.   *(67th/68th)*   *212-861-3100*

This cowboy store has always felt a bit out of place on Madison Avenue; one look at the price tags will help make the connection. Billy Martin's is known for its exquisite line of hand-crafted cowboy boots that are available in various colors and patterns. Urban cowgirls can add country-western flair to their wardrobes with suede jackets and wrap skirts, fitted cowboy shirts, gorgeous hand-beaded belts, turquoise jewelry, and belt buckles.

· *Suede skirt $595*

· **Billy Martin's** · **Char** · **For Joseph** · **Jan Faulkner**
· **Lone Pine** · **Manuel** · **Stallion** · **Stubbs**

☺ M-F 10-7, Sat 10-6, Sun 12-5
Store credit w/ receipt.

B- | A- | A- |

Max Mara
813 Madison Ave.   *(@ 68th)*   *212-879-6100*

This recently revamped Italian line makes beautiful clothing for women in search of clothes with an elegant, Italian-movie-star feel. Selections include cashmere and camel-hair suits in diverse color palettes. The cuts are generous and the fabrics are exceptional.

· *Camel winter coats $1200*

· **Max Mara** · **S Collection** · **Sportmax Weekend**

☺ M-T 10-6, W-F 10-7, Sat 10-6
Store credit w/in 5 days w/ receipt.

B- | A- | A+ |

U P P E R   E A S T   S I D E

Malo
814 Madison Ave.   *(@ 68th)*   *212-396-4721*

If you are looking for chunky cashmere sweaters—and you have deep pockets—Malo will be a heavenly experience. Cashmere doesn't come cheap anywhere, but Malo's gives you quality for the price. And don't miss the long, drapey trousers and skirts, which look great when paired with the knee-length sweater coats.

· *2-ply cashmere sweater $610*

· **Malo**

☺ M-Sat 10-6, Th 10-7
Store credit w/in 10 days w/ receipt.

   B- | **B+** | **A+** |

Versace
815 Madison Ave.   *(68th/69th)*   *212-744-6868*

It's not the same without Gianni at the helm, but it will do. Donatella is all about glitz and glam, from the sexy, outrageous dresses down to the slinky, strappy shoes. Walking into this boutique will remind you of the days of the supermodel, when excess reigned and glamour ruled.

· *Evening gowns $2500-$10,000*

· **Versace**

☺ M-Sat 10-6, Th 10-7
Store credit w/in 5 days w/ receipt.

   C- | **A+** | **A+** |

Joan & David
816 Madison Ave.   *(68th/69th)*   *212-772-3970*

This simple and conservative boutique is known primarily for its shoes, which are trend-conscious without being trendy. The coats and suits lean towards the traditional both in color and cut. Basics that would elsewhere be boring become elegant essentials at Joan & David, thanks to the fine quality of the merchandise.

· *Silver snake shoes $240*

· **Joan & David**

☺ M-Sat 10-6
Refund w/in 10 days. Sale items final.

   B+ | **B** | **A** | (3)

Oilily
820 Madison Ave.   *(68th/69th)*   *212-772-8686*

All year round, Oilily carries great beachwear which can take you from Bridgehampton to the Bahamas to Bali (this store knows that its clientele gets around). You can also find baby tees and colorful, patterned sarong-style skirts. The down-to-earth sales people provide a friendly atmosphere and make shopping the pleasant experience it's supposed to be.

· *Sarong skirts $221*

· **Oilily**

☺ M-Sat 10-6, Th 10-7, Sun 12-5
Store credit w/in 14 days.
Will send check for full refund.

   B+ | **B** | **A-** |

MADISON AVENUE

Loro Piana
821 Madison Ave.   *(68th/69th)*   *212-980-7961*

It may be stuffy and conservative, but Loro Piana remains one of the best-quality boutiques in Manhattan. The world-renowned mill produces fine cashmere products that appeal to financially established women. **Best Find: Cashmere slippers $195.**

· *Printed cashmere shawls $1650*
· **Loro Piana**
☺ M-Sat 10-6
Store credit w/in 15 days.

C+		A-		A+	

Dolce & Gabbana
825 Madison Ave.   *(68th/69th)*   *212-249-4100*

This partnership rose to prominence in the late 80s, and it still evokes a Donald Trump-like spirit of shameless excess. From dramatic black evening dresses with built-in bustiers ornamented with butterflies and flowers to beaded and rhinestoned capri pants, the clothes are glitzy, glamorous and fun.

· *Open-toe heels $400*
· **Dolce & Gabbana**
☺ T-Sat 10-6, Th 10-7
Store credit w/in 10 days w/ receipt.

C		A		A+	

TSE Cashmere
827 Madison Ave.   *(@ 69th)*   *212-472-7790*

The TSE line is known for modern, chic clothing for urban women. Cashmere twin sets are now available here in an array of colors that make your mouth water. The generous cuts mean that the sweaters are more boxy than snug. The prices are not exorbitant for cashmere, but they are rather high, so hold out for the bi-annual sample sale if you can.

· *Twinset $550*
· **TSE Cashmere** · **TSE New York**
☺ M-Sat 10-6, Th 10-7
Refund w/in 30 days w/ receipt.

C		A-		A	

Sergio Rossi
835 Madison Ave.   *(69th/70th)*   *212-396-4814*

At Sergio Rossi, the simple black shoe does not exist. Instead, outrageous styles, like beaded and embroidered blue suede knee-length boots, vie for your attention. Fine shoes never come cheap, and Sergio Rossi is no exception, but in these shoes you will definitely have people asking after your feet.

· *Orange and turquoise embroidered and beaded*
  cashmere stiletto boots $1110
· **Sergio Rossi**
☺ M-Sat 10-6
Store credit w/in 10 days.

C+		A-		A	

service | presentation | quality | expense

UPPER EAST SIDE

Prada
841 Madison Ave.   *(@ 70th)*   *212-327-4200*

Go for the nylon bags. True, you're shelling out $400 for a piece of parachute, but the bags are truly sleek, classic, oddly elegant, and durable. The Prada symbol will carry you into the millennium, with clothing that manages to balance fashion-forward styles with classic cuts to produce a modern aesthetic that is flawless. The Italian loafers are also must-haves and the sweaters in beautiful dark grays and blacks are welcome staples. **Best Find: Olive leather/wool chest bag with fur pocket $590.**

· *Nylon/parachute tote bag $490*

· **Prada · Prada Sport**

☺ M-Sat 10-6, Th 10-7
Store credit w/in 10 days w/ tags and receipt.

C | A | A+ |

Gianfranco Ferre
845 Madison Ave.   *(@ 70th)*   *212-717-5430*

Gianfranco Ferre designs an iconoclastic line of couture and ready-to-wear clothes for sophisticated Manhattanites that may resuscitate those bored to death by contemporary fashion. From a suit with flair to a dramatic tafetta gown, a Ferre outfit delivers sheer style.

· *Scalloped patent leather wedge shoe $370*

· **Gianfranco Ferre**

☺ M-Sat 10-6
Store credit or exchange w/ receipt.

B- | A- | A+ |

Chlöe
850 Madison Ave.   *(@ 70th)*   *212-717-8220*

The boutique is a masterpiece in itself, with a winding marble staircase coaxing you upstairs to the fabulous fashions. Since Stella McCartney has begun designing for the line, Chlöe has refocused on a younger, more chic generation and now features everything from fully beaded tank-tops to silk denim jeans.

· *Beaded spaghetti strap top $1300*

· **Chlöe**

☺ M-Sat 10-6
Refunds w/ receipt.

C+ | A | A+ |

Jennifer Tyler
854 Madison Ave.   *(@ 70th)*   *212-772-8350*

This location houses Tyler's more upscale collection of cashmeres. The rainbow of hues displayed in the window will draw you toward the selection of sweaters from pullovers to twinsets. The super-soft shawls, scarves, and gloves make excellent gifts.

· *Fitted cashmere cardigan with pearl buttons $185*

· **Brunello Lucinelli · Jennifer Tyler · John Lang**
· **Lombarda Lassani**

☺ M-Sat 10-6, Sun 12-6
Store credit w/ receipt. Sale items final.

C+ | A- | A |

find these stores @ www.fyifashion.com   **21**

service | presentation | quality | expense

MADISON AVENUE

Sonia Rykiel
849 Madison Ave.   *(70th/71st)*   212-396-3060

This French designer made her mark in fashion with her velours. Today the clothing is a bit more eccentric and expensive and seems geared to a mature crowd. However, younger shoppers may be drawn to Rykiel's occasional fresh take on an old favorite, such as a well-done black sweater or leopard-print rainboots. **Best Find: Leopard print rain boots $90.**

· *Cashmere sweater $800*

· **Sonia Rykiel**

☺ M-Sat 10-6
Store credit w/in 2-3 days w/ receipt.

C+ | B+ | A |

Yves Saint Laurent
855 Madison Ave.   *(70th/71st)*   212-472-5299

You don't have to pay admission to browse at this world-famous fashion house, but you do need serious cash to actually buy any of the beautiful clothing. If you've got a trust fund, a sugar daddy, or a great job, spring for a killer couture suit. And don't forget to pick up some footwear in the less-formal shoe salon.

· *Suit $2500*

· **Yves Saint Laurent**

☺ M-Sat 10-6
Store credit w/in 10 days w/ receipt.

B+ | A- | A+ |

Equipment
872 Madison Ave.   *(@ 71st)*   212-249-2083

Exquisitely-made button-down shirts used to be the narrow focus of this French boutique. Unfortunately, its expanded line of dresses, pants, and sweaters doesn't compare in originality. The selection is sparse and the prices are high.

· *Cotton oxford $125*

· **Equipment**

☺ M-Sat 10-6, Sun 12-5
Store credit w/in 10 days.

B | B | A- |

Ralph Lauren
867 Madison Ave.   *(@ 72nd)*   212-606-2100

This store will never go out of style. All the floors of the gorgeously restored Rhinelander mansion are filled with flawlessly designed clothing, from perfectly tailored trousers to classically elegant evening gowns to vintage leather jackets. Of course, everything will cost a pretty penny, but even those with slender wallets should at least take a tour. A girl can dream, can't she?

· *Cashmere sweaters $900*

· **Ralph Lauren Black Label** · **Ralph Lauren Collection**
· **RL by Ralph Lauren**

☺ M-Sat 10-6, Th 10-8
Refund w/in 30 days w/ receipt.

C+ | A+ | A+ |

service | presentation | quality | expense

Polo Sport
888 Madison Ave.   *(@ 72nd)*   *212-434-8000*

This multi-level store features more affordable, practical sportswear than the landmark mansion across the street. From the classic flag sweaters in a variety of knits and colors to the adorable hooded sweatshirts in khaki, navy, and orange, these clothes make the perfect addition to any urban wardrobe.

· *Kid's size orange hooded sweatshirt $95*

· **Polo Golf** · **Polo Ralph Lauren** · **Polo Sport**
· **Polo Sportsman/Sportswoman** · **Polo Tennis**
· **Ralph Lauren Collection** · **RLX**

☺ M-Sat 10-6, Th 10-8
Refund w/in 30 days.

    C+ | B+ | A- |

Portantina
895 Madison Ave.   *(@ 72nd)*   *212-472-0636*

This teensy-weensy, dark, bohemian boutique is filled with a luxurious inventory of clothing made in velvets and fine wools that will please tactile freaks. The store is also a veritable treasure trove of fabulous scarves and shawls; and it's even better for unusual evening bags.

· *Velvet shawls $675*

· **Hanna Hartnell** · **Portantina** · **Susan Unger**

☺ M-Sat 10:30-6, Sun 12-5
Store credit w/in 10 days.

    B- | B | A |

Bra Smyth
905 Madison Ave.   *(72nd/73rd)*   *212-772-9400*

This well-stocked lingerie boutique carries everything from sexy little bras and teddies to cozy PJs and robes. Whether you need to stock up on the bare essentials or are just looking for a lush bathrobe, drop in and check it out.

· *Furry bathrobe $236*

· **Chantal Thomas** · **Lise Charmelle** · **Simone Perele** · **Timpa**

☺ M-Sat 10-7
Exchange w/in 14 days.

    C+ | B- | B+ |

Calypso St. Barth
935 Madison Ave.   *(74th/75th)*   *212-535-4100*

Think pink! Also blue, and green, yellow, red, orange and purple. Black is banned at this trend-setting Caribbean boutique, where goods are arranged according to the colors of the rainbow. Add some spice to an otherwise drab wardrobe from the shop's endless supply of bright, original pieces. The bags, scarves and other items will leave you swooning.

· *Corduroy bustle skirt $140*

· **3 Dots** · **Anna K** · **Beautiful People** · **Brooklyn Handknits**
· **Calypso** · **Coup de Pied** · **Diab'less** · **Dosa** · **Lluis**
· **Maletesta** · **Matilde** · **Miguelena** · **Paul & Joe**

☺ M-Sat 11-7, Sun 12-6
Store credit w/in 10 days w/ receipt.

    B | A- | A- |

MADISON AVENUE

Christian Louboutin
941 Madison Ave.   (74th/75th)   212-396-1884

Both the décor and the selection would qualify this as the perfect spot for the Mad Hatter to shop, had the Mad Hatter been a woman with a shoe fetish. Though the outrageous styles, like thigh-high camouflage boots, verge on unwearable, the right occasion just might warrant a pair of these very expensive shoes.

· *Camouflage knee-high boots $1200*

· **Christian Louboutin**

☺ M-Sat 10-6
Store credit w/in 7 days w/ receipt.

B	A+	A	

Cashmere Cashmere
965 Madison Ave.   (75th/76th)   212-988-5252

Definitely one of the better-quality cashmere stores in New York, Cashmere Cashmere carries all styles of sweaters—fitted or loose—and caters to the shamelessly self-indulgent. The color range is exceptional, from bold red and orange to classic navy and black, but you won't find any bargains except the gloves, which make good gifts. **Best Find: Gloves $50**.

· *Twinset: shell $495, cardigan $695*

· **Cashmere Cashmere**

☺ M-Sat 10-6, Sun 12-5
Store credit w/in 14 days w/ receipt.

A-	B+	A	

En Soie
988 Madison Ave.   (@ 77th)   212-717-7958

Colorful outfits are available at this prim and proper store, which features a consistent line of shirts, poufy skirts, and pants in silk and other luxury fabrics. The silk capri pants with matching shirts make great casual evening outfits when the weather's warm. **Best Find: Cotton pants $140**.

· *Silk coat $1100*

· **En Soie**

☺ M-Sat 10-6
Store credit or exchange.

B	B+	A-	

Vera Wang
991 Madison Ave.   (@ 77th)   212-628-3400

Vera Wang has expanded her line to include a collection of evening gowns that are as exquisite as her notoriously beautiful wedding dresses. Intricate beading on luxurious fabrics and flattering cuts can make anyone wearing a Vera Wang dress stand out in the crowd even if she's not the bride! Make an appointment.

· *Evening dresses $3,000-$10,000*

· **Vera Wang**

☺ By appt. only. Open house Th 6-7
Evening wear and cocktail dresses
returnable w/out alterations w/in 2-3 days.

A-	A+	A+	

service | presentation | quality | expense

Issey Miyake
992 Madison Ave.   *(@ 77th)*   212-439-7822

Clothing may be art—but is art clothing? How you answer that question will determine how you feel about Miyake's clothes. His garments feature extreme details like hula-hoop hemlines, gargantuan funnel necks, or sashes with pom-poms the size of your head.

· *Pleated tops $300*

· **Issey Miyake**

☺ M-F 10-6, Sat 11-6
Store credit w/in 7 days.

C+ | A- | A |

Alicia Mugetti
999 Madison Ave.   *(77th/78th)*   212-794-6186

At Alicia Mugetti, the dressed mannequins always look as if they've stepped out of a Midsummer Night's Dream. The romantic dresses are crushed satin or velvet and bring out a woman's most feminine side. In the very back of the store are simple thin velvet dresses in beautiful colors—the store's best feature.

· *Floor-length velvet dress $650*

· **Alicia Mugetti**

☺ M-Sat 10-6
Store credit w/in 10 days.

C | A- | A |

Intermix
1003 Madison Ave.   *(77th/78th)*   212-249-7858

For those who remember the ghosts of Madison Avenue past, Intermix will conjure visions of Charivari. This European-style store is for the shopper who is a little less faddish yet a little more daring. Dangling beaded hemlines, colorful ponchos and a large selection of decorative bags fill the place.

· *Jamin Puech bags $300*

· **Alberta Ferretti** · **Amy Chan** · **Anna Sui** · **Catherine**
· **Chaiken & Capone** · **D&G** · **Daryl K** · **Earl Jeans**
· **Helmut Lang** · **Intermix** · **Jamin Puech** · **John Bartlett**
· **Joseph** · **Katayone Adeli** · **Kate Spade** · **Nikki B** · **Paul & Joe**
· **Plein Sud** · **Raffe** · **Rebecca Dannenberg** · **Rebecca Taylor**
· **Siegerson Morrison** · **Stella Pace** · **Theory** · **Tocca**
· **Tracy Feith** · **Vivienne Tam** · **Vivienne Westwood** · **William B**

☺ M-Sat 10-7, Sun 12-6
Store credit w/in 10 days.

C+ | A- | A- |

René Collections
1007 Madison Ave.   *(77th/78th)*   212-327-3912

Handbags for the more conservative woman fill this accessory boutique. For a top-notch original or a knockoff that might even fool the experts, René Collections has a lot to offer. The store also houses a fine selection of leather wallets and belts.

· *Jackie O. bag copy $315*

· **René**

☺ M-Sat 9:30-6:30, Sun 12-5
Store credit w/in 7 days.

C+ | B- | A- |

service | presentation | quality | expense

Missoni
1009 Madison Ave.   (@ 78th)   212-517-9339

This famous Italian line, with its gorgeous Madison Avenue store, has been revamped, and it now features handbags, classic Missoni-print string bikinis, and (for splurging) cowl-neck sweaters. The space is several times larger than necessary, but this exquisite wearable art is worth the extra time you'll spend walking from rack to rack.

· *Cowl-neck sweaters $465*

· **Missoni**

☺ M-Sat 10-6
Store credit w/in 10 days w/ receipt.

C+ | A | A+ |

Luca Luca
1011 Madison Ave.   (@ 78th)   212-288-9285

Though catering to a mature, wealthier clientele, Luca Luca offers several items for the hipper, younger Manhattanite: fitted wool coats styled à la Audrey Hepburn in the winter, and beautiful, flowing chiffon blouses and evening gowns in summer.

· *Pané velvet dress, $1800*

· **Luca Luca**

☺ M-Sat 10-6:30, Th 10-8
Store credit w/ receipt.

B- | B | A+ |

Midali
1015 Madison Ave.   (78th/79th)   212-879-2563

Mature women who want to wear contemporary fashion instead of frumpy frocks can find an interesting mix of clothes at Midali. The cuts are on the conservative side but the clothes have European flair and the colors and patterns give them real personality.

· *Wool suit $910*

· **Martino Midali**

☺ M-Sat 10-6
Store credit w/in 7 days.

B+ | B+ | A- |

Michael's
1041 Madison Ave., 2nd Floor (79th/80th)   212-737-7273

At Michael's, speed is the key and strength of character is a must. The discouraging "I couldn't care less" attitude of the sales staff is nothing short of scary, and if you dare to bring in resale goods you'll have to deal with the Soup Nazi of consignment. When she sizes up your merchandise with her unmerciful gaze, you'll feel as if she's passing judgement on your soul. But if you've got the mettle, you can find some great bargains here, like $40 Hermès scarves.

· *Chanel suit $700*

Frequently features: Chanel · Dolce & Gabbana · Donna Karan · Giorgio Armani · Gucci · Hermès · Prada · Valentino

☺ M-Sat 9:30-6, Th 9:30-8
All sales final.

D- | C+ | A- |

U P P E R   E A S T   S I D E

La Boutique Resale
1045 Madison Ave., 2nd Floor (79th/80th) 212-517-8099

The friendly sales staff is helpful and fiercely proud of offering virtually new designer goods such as Chanel, Yves Saint Laurent, and Donna Karan. You alone will know that the item you purchased once hung in someone else's closet.

· *Valentino short skirt $75*

Frequently features: Agnès B. · Chanel · Dana Buchman · Dolce & Gabbana · Escada · Fendi · Giorgio Armani · Issey Miyake · Moschino · Prada · Valentino · Versace · YSL

☺ M-Sat 11-7, Th 11-8, Sun 12-6
All sales final.

| B+ | B | A- | |

Agnès B.
1063 Madison Ave.   (80th/81st)   212-570-9333

Agnès B. has captured simple Parisian style and brought it effortlessly to New York. Agnès B. basics have looked the same for over 15 years and they still mix into a woman's wardrobe as if they were conceived of yesterday.

· *Cotton cardigan t-shirt $45*

· **Agnès B.**

☺ M-Sat 11-7, Sun 12-6
Store credit w/in 10 days.

| C+ | B+ | B- | |

Olive & Bette's
1070 Madison Ave.   (80th/81st)   212-717-9655

This adorable shop has come a long way from its earlier Westside-only location. Once featuring exclusively young and excessively trendy merchandise, Olive & Bette's now has a reputation for being a well-stocked source of fun clothing that's hip for all ages.

· *Cotton skirt $250*

· **Bette Paige · Bisou Bisou · Claudine Penedo · Diab'less · Diane Von Furstenberg · Diesel · Earl Jeans · Easel · Free People · JET · Jill Stuart · Juicy Couture · Katayone Adeli · Le Havlin Piro · Michael Stars · Miguelena · Olive & Bette · Petro Zillia · Shoshanna · Susanna Monaco · Theory · Vivienne Tam · William B**

☺ M-Sat 11-7, Sun 11-6
Store credit w/in 7 days w/ tags.

| A- | A- | A- | |

Franceska
1070 Madison Ave.   (@ 81st)   212-744-5400

This boutique mixes current European-chic with longtime classics. Crammed with designer labels and carrying everything from tight-fitting pants to more traditional suits, the store is ideal for mothers and daughters on a shopping excursion together. **Best Find: Wool shawl $100**.

· *Suit $400*

· **Anti-Flirt · Cecile Jeanne · Elita · Friponne · Hanky Panky · Levante · LM Lulu · Morgan · On Gossamer**

☺ M-Sat 11-7, Sun 12-6
Store credit w/in 7 days.

| A | B | A- | |

MADISON AVENUE

Rapax

1100 Madison Ave.   (82nd/83rd)   212-734-5171

Rapax carries a good selection of classic shoes while staying abreast of current fashion. Upper East Siders who want to break out of Gucci loafer-land but aren't ready for ruby slippers should check out the large selection of flats and simple evening pumps.

· *Camel leather ballet flats $165*

· **Claudio Merazzi · Giorgio Moretto · Pancaldi · Rapax**
· **Roberto Rinaldi · Tremp**

☺ M-Sat 10-7, Sun 11-5
Store credit.

| **B+** | **B-** | **A-** | |

Cashmere New York

1100 Madison Ave.   (82nd/83rd)   212-744-3500

Ballroom skirts with cashmere twin-sets are what's happening, and here's where you'll find the sweaters year round—in pastel shades in summer, jewel tones in winter.

· *Rhinestone and silk skirt $650*

· **Cashmere New York**

☺ M-Sat 10-6
Store credit w/in 10 days w/ receipt.

| **C-** | **B+** | **A** | |

Anik

1122 Madison Ave.   (83rd/84th)   212-249-2417

The Madison Avenue location offers the best pieces from each collection and the wall-length cubby area is filled with a seemingly infinite supply of tops. Wear a suit to work and then whip off the jacket on your way out of the office to reveal the tank underneath.

· *Theory jean jacket $175*

· **Bianca Nero · Chaiken & Capone · Easel · Index**
· **Isabel Ardee · Jill Stuart · Juicy Couture · Kostum**
· **Page 3 · Susanna Monaco · Teen Flo · Theory · Urchin**
· **Velvet · Yigal Azrouel**

☺ M-Sat 10-8 Sun 11-7
Store credit w/in 7 days w/ tags & receipt.

| **B-** | **A** | **A-** | |

Encore

1132 Madison Ave., 2nd Floor (84th/85th) 212-879-2850

This is the Upper East Side's best kept secret. Encore is a resale shop filled with high-end designer labels in exceptional condition. The shop is as well-organized as any Madison Avenue boutique, so you won't feel like you're at the Grace Church rummage sale as you search for the perfect Chanel suit or pair of Ralph Lauren pants.

· *Chanel cap-sleeve cashmere sweater $180*

· **Alexander McQueen · Azzedine Alaïa · Bill Blass · Celine**
· **Chanel · Chlöe · Dolce & Gabbana · Donna Karan**
· **Emanuel Ungaro · Fendi · Givenchy · Gucci · Helmut Lang**
· **Hermès · Issey Miyake · Jil Sander · Lagerfeld · Lanvin**
· **Marc Jacobs · Michael Kors · Oscar de la Renta · Prada**
· **Ralph Lauren · Thierry Mugler · Vera Wang · Yohji Yamamoto**

☺ M-F 10:30-6:30, Sat 10:30-6, Sun 12-6
All sales final.

| **A** | **B+** | **A-** | |

Bis
1134 Madison Ave., 2nd Floor (84th/85th) 212-396-2760

Divorces, eating disorders, bad shopping judgement: donors' misfortunes become customers' good luck at Bis, where resale is as upscale as it gets and every piece of clothing has a story to tell. Couture pieces are sold on consignment, and any given day a perfect-condition Chanel suit could fall into your hands at thirty percent of the retail value. The evening dress and accessories selection is even better.

· *Chanel suit $1000*

· **Chanel · Gucci · Hermès · Prada · Tod's · Valentino**

☺ M-Th 10-7, F-Sat 10-6, Sun 12-5
All sales final.

A | **B+** | **A** | 3

Diana & Jeffries
1145 Madison Ave.   (@ 85th)   212-249-1891

Though the exterior is a little shabby and out of date, the clothing is anything but. Diana & Jeffries showcases the hottest lines in town. Younger women who want up-to-the-minute mainstream fashion should definitely pencil this store into their shopping itineraries.

· *Short knit skirt by Nell, $98*

· **3 Dots · 614 · ABS · Alice & Trixie · Bella Dahl · Bette Paige**
· **Big Star · Buzz 18 · Catherine · Central Park West · Easel**
· **For Joseph · Iris Singer · Jane Doe · Jenne Maag**
· **Juicy Couture · Margaret O'Leary · Michael Stars**
· **Nanette Lepore · Nell · NKL · Petit Bateau · Shoshanna**
· **Supply & Demand · Tease Tees · Theory · Todd Oldham**
· **Urchin · Vivienne Tam · White & Warren**

☺ M-Sat 11-7, Sun 12-6
Store credit w/in 14 days w/ receipt.

B- | **B-** | **A-** | 3

Fopp's
1265 Madison Ave.   (90th/91st)   212-831-3432

The less-than-stellar exterior belies the high caliber of the goods inside. Fopp's in an excellent store for mature, conservative women and carries casual attire from upper-echelon designers.

· *Suit $600*

· **Agatha · Anti-Flirt · Courrèges · Entracte · Patrick Mendes**
· **Surabaya · Toupy**

☺ M-F 10-6:30, Sat 10-6
Store credit w/in 7 days w/ receipt.

A- | **B-** | **A** | 4

The Original Levi's Store
750 Lexington Ave.   (@ 60th)   212-826-5957

The blue jeans hardly need mentioning, but Levi's is an enormous store that has all the basics covered. The T-shirts, button-downs, khakis, and jean jackets are sure to last, though we all know that nothing will stand the test of time like the 501 Blues.

· *501 Jeans $54*

· **Levi's**

☺ M-Sat 10-8, Sun 12-6
Refund w/ receipt. Store credit w/outut.

C+ | **B** | **B+** | 2

LEXINGTON AVENUE

Diesel
770 Lexington Ave.   (@ 60th)   212-308-0055

It's hard to make old fashion news exciting, but Diesel, which sells mainly jeans, has managed to do so. The flagship store, which feels more like a large submarine than an East Side shop, offers great cuts and a variety of materials. If you can't commit to another pair of jeans, check out the urban streetwear on the second floor.

· *Diesel Jeans $125*

· **Diesel** · **Diesel Style Lab**

☺ M-Sat 10-8, Sun 12-6
Refund w/in 21 days w/ receipt and tags.

    B+ | **B+** | **A-** |

Maraolo
782 Lexington Ave.   (@ 61st)   212-832-8182

The quintessential Upper East Side shoe spot, Maraolo specializes in classic casual styles. Reasonably priced loafers in durable leathers are its trademark. Occasionally the store features a knock-out pair of sandals that shouldn't be passed up.

· *Very high red velvet wedge sandals $290*

· **Coca** · **Maraolo**

☺ M-Sat 10-8, Sun 12:30-6
Exchange anytime.

    B- | **B-** | **A-** |

Ashanti
872 Lexington Ave.   (65th/66th)   212-535-0740

Stylish plus-size fashions are hard to come by in Manhattan, which makes Ashanti a priceless treasure. The store carries fashionable clothing from sizes 14 to 32. The clothes are made from luxury fabrics like silks and knits, and the styles are dramatic and chic. If a particular item catches your eye but doesn't come in your size, Ashanti will special-order it for you.

· *Cotton knit dress w/ hood $176*

· **Barbara McCaine for Ashanti** · **Coco & Juan** · **Flax Generous**
· **Stephanie Schuster** · **Vicki Vi**

☺ M-Sat 10-6, Th 10-8, Sun 12-5
Refund except on sale and one-of-a-kind items.

    B+ | **B-** | **B+** |

Cinco
960 Lexington Ave.   (@ 70th)   212-794-3826

Crammed with trendy labels, Cinco carries fashionable clothes for both work and play. Though nothing here is original or a steal, the compact selection makes choosing a breeze.

· *Tark pants $225*

· **3 Dots** · **Earl Jeans** · **Easel** · **Icon** · **James Perse**
· **Juicy Couture** · **Michael Stars** · **Tark** · **Theory** · **Vertigo**

☺ M-F 10-7, Sat 11-7, Sun 12-6:30
Store credit w/in 7 days w/ receipt.
Sale items final.

    C+ | **B-** | **A-** |

service | presentation | quality | expense

Vincent & Edgar
972 Lexington Ave.   (70th/71st)   212-288-4205

This custom shoe store will make any shoe your pretty little (or not so little) feet desire, in whatever style you can dream up. Vincent & Edgar is particularly great for irregular sizes, or hard-to-find large and small sizes. A custom shoe doesn't come cheap, though.

· *Custom shoes $1500*

· **Vincent & Edgar**

☺ M-F 10-5 by appt. only
All sales final.

B		B		A-	

San Francisco Clothing Company
975 Lexington Ave.   (70th/71st)   212-472-8740

This store has been around for quite some time, but its drab exterior keeps it from being noticed. The fashions within are conservatively elegant and perfect for stylish moms, who can conveniently shop for their kids while they peruse the button-down shirts and straight velvet skirts in grown-up sizes. **Best Find: Velvet strapless "tube" top $295**.

· *Cotton oxford shirt $145*

· **August Silk · Central Park West · Jonden**
· **San Francisco Clothing Company**

☺ M-Sat 11-6
Store credit w/in 10 days w/ receipt.

C+		B-		A-	

Betsey Bunky Nini
980 Lexington Ave.   (71st/72nd)   212-744-6716

A cool place for baby-boomers to shop. The clothes prove that a mature woman can dress her age and still look hip. A great place to find many styles of pant and skirt suits, some formal wear, and a fantastic selection of casual wear. **Best Find: Paul Smith skirt suit $1458**.

· *Suit $1000*

· **Alberta Ferretti · Cividini · Gunext · Paul Smith**
· **Peter Cohen · Piazza Sempione**

☺ M-Sat 10:30-6, Th 10:30-7, Sun 12-5
Store credit w/in 10 days.

A		B+		A-	

French Sole
985 Lexington Ave.   (71st/72nd)   212-737-2859

For adult women who have never quite recovered from ballerina fantasies, French Sole offers consolation. Its delicate ballet flats come in every color and pattern a girl could dream up. The charming selection also includes lots of other feminine footwear, like sequined Chinese slippers and embroidered wool clogs. **Best Find: Sequined Chinese-style slipper $105**.

· *Ballet flat $95*

· **Arcopedico · Dansko · Frankie & Baby · French Sole**
· **Hirica · Love & Desire · Superga**

☺ M-F 10-7, Sat 11-6
Store credit or exchange w/in 7 days w/ receipt.

C+		B-		B+	

LEXINGTON AVENUE

Danielle B.
1034 Lexington Ave.   (73rd/74th)   212-772-8153

This non-descript boutique carries a random selection of merchandise ranging from very conservative suits to cozy wool sweaters in vibrant colors. The selection depends completely on when you go, making it a hit-or-miss shopping experience.

· *Skirt $700-$1000*

· **Apara** · **BP Studio** · **Martine Douvier** · **Poles** · **Rodika** · **Tehen** · **Zanian**

☺ M-F 10:30-6:30, Sat 10:30-6
Store credit, receipt preferred.

| C | C- | A- | 4 |

Sylvia Pine's Uniquities
1102 Lexington Ave.   (77th/78th)   212-744-5141

These handbags really make you appreciate the craftsmanship of the past. The beaded and petit-point items in Silvia Pine's collection date back to the Victorian era and have been fully restored. Buy one as an evening bag for special occasions, or start a collection of your own. They make great wall decorations.

· *Petit-point evening bag $250*

· **N/A**

☺ Tu-Sat 10-5
All sales final unless it's a gift. Gifts can be exchanged.

| A- | A- | A | 3 |

Nara
1132 Lexington Ave.   (78th/79th)   212-628-1577

Is $2400 too much to spend on a leather bag? Nara thinks so. That's why they have designer imitations for under $200. The quality is great and the replicas are amazing, so be sure to stop in and pick up a bogus Tod's.

· *Focus bag (Tod's style) $169*

· **Focus** · **M. London** · **Stefano Bravo**

☺ M-F 11-7, Sat 11-6
Exchange only. Evening wear sales final.

| C+ | C+ | B+ | 2 |

Forreal Basics
1200 Lexington Ave.   (81st/82nd)   212-717-0493

The store itself is rather unappealing, but Forreal Basics manages to stuff every nook and cranny with the most popular tees and jeans. While it's targeted to the younger set, Forreal Basics may also offer up some items that may interest mom.

· *Mavi Jeans $55*

· **Diab'less** · **Mavi** · **Michael Stars** · **Petit Bateau** · **Polo Sport**

☺ M-Sat 11-7, Sun 12-6
Store credit any time.

| C+ | C+ | B | 2 |

service | presentation | quality | expense

Bloomingdale's
1000 Third Ave.   *(@ 59th)*   212-705-2000

After a grueling day of boutique hopping, you begin to appreciate the lateral convenience of department store shopping. Coming out of a several-year style slump, Bloomingdale's is back at the top of its game. It carries virtually all of the popular high-fashion labels under one roof.

· *Katayone Adeli black slacks $149*

Labels include: BCBG · Chlöe · Cynthia Steffe · Dana Buchman · Daryl K · Donna Karan Collection · Easel · Emanuel Ungaro · French Connection · Helmut Lang · Hourglass · Juicy Couture · Karl Lagerfeld · Lacoste · Laundry · Madison Brown · Max Studio · Michael Stars · Parallel · Polo Sport · Ralph by Ralph Lauren · Sonia Rykiel · St. John · Tessuto · Theory · Trina Turk · TSE Cashmere · Vera Wang · William B.

☺ M-F 10-8:30, Sat 10-7, Sun 11-7
Varies w/ department.

    C+ | B | A- |

Martier
1010 Third Ave.   *(@ 60th)*   212-758-5370

For girls who just wanna have fun, Martier has colorful frocks for evening, from mini-dresses with cowl necks in red stretch velvet to full skirts in vivid colors with matching front-laced corsets. Even the daytime apparel makes a statement in the form of pashmina knee-length skirts and plain black pants spruced up with embroidery and rhinestone cumberbunds. Don't get distracted by the close proximity of Bloomingdale's. Martier has it one-upped in the partywear department.

· *Vertigo black pants with embroidered waistband $200*

· Aubade · Christies · Helen Wang · Helena Sorrel · Juan Carlos Piñera · La Perla · Lise Charmelle · Mandalay · Morgan de Toi · Rebecca Taylor · Sharagano · Ticci Tonetto · Vertigo · Vertigo · William B

☺ M-Sat 10-8, Sun 12:30-6
Store credit w/in 14 days with receipt.

   B- | B+ | B+ |

Martinez Valero
1029 Third Ave.   *(@ 61st)*   212-753-1822

The obscenely reasonable prices make it easy to talk yourself into buying both the faux snakeskin sling-backs and loafer-esque mutations with short squared-off toes. The styles here are just the right mix of classic, funk, and edginess to be appealing to all women. **Best Find: Stretch velvet knee-high boots $142**.

· *Gabaradine loafer with patent heel $145*

· Martinez Valero

☺ M-F 10-8, Sat 11-7, Sun 12-6
Store credit w/in 14 days w/ receipt.

    C+ | B+ | B+ | (2)

service | presentation | quality | expense

Chuckies
1073 Third Ave.   *(63rd/64th)*   212-593-9898

This shoe boutique looks more like a Park Avenue living room, but carries a great selection of popular European brands. Animal print stilettos or nylon ankle boots are among the stylish items you might find here. Chuckies also has a small selection of outrageous bags.

· *Chuckies ankle boots $235*

· **Alberto Guardini · Casadei · Costume National**
· **Cynthia Rowley · David Ackerman · Dolce & Gabbana**
· **Ernesto Esposito · Jimmy Choo · L'Autre Chose · Le Silla**
· **Miu Miu · Moda Italia · Patrick Cox · Pollini · Prada Sport**
· **Sergio Rossi · Studio Pollini**

☺ M-Sat 10:45-7:45, Sun 12:30-5:30
Store credit w/in 14 days w/ receipt.

B | B- | A |

Club Monaco
1111 Third Ave.   *(@ 65th)*   212-355-2949

Calvin Klein minimalism meets Soho chic at Club Monaco, where sleek, fashionable clothing is affordable. The clothes range from a variety of high-fashion-type suits and dresses to sporty active wear.

· *Wool pants $89*

· **Club Monaco**

☺ M-Sat 11-7, Sun 12-5
Refund anytime. Sale items final.

A- | B+ | A- |

Bebe
1127 Third Ave.   *(@ 66th)*   212-935-2444

The merchandise here verges on over-the-top, but if you comb through it patiently, you can almost always find a couple of exceptional pieces, such as a leather racing jacket or a cashmere twin-set, that won't cost you a week's salary.

· *Long-sleeve gauze shirt $79*

· **Bebe**

☺ M-F 10-8, Sat 10-7, Sun 11-6
Refund w/in 14 days w/ tags and receipt.

C+ | B | B |

Scoop
1277 Third Ave.   *(73rd/74th)*   212-744-3380

It seems like Scoop is taking over the Upper East Side. The expanding (adjacent) boutiques carry the most feminine fashions without being enslaved to trends. Color is the key in this store, where the clothes are a combination of Upper East Side sophistication and downtown cool with an ethnic influence.

· *Earl suede jeans $520*

· **Blumarine · Chaiken & Capone · D&G · Daryl K**
· **Diane Von Furstenberg · Earl Jeans · Easel · Ghost · Inca**
· **Jimmy Choo · Katayone Adeli · Michael Kors · Petit Bateau**
· **Shoshanna · Theory · Tocca · TSE Cashmere · William B**

☺ M-F 11-8, Sat 11-7, Sun 12-6
Store credit w/in 14 days.

A- | A | A |

Vivaldi

1288 Third Ave.   (@ 74th)   212-734-2805

From the window display, you might get the impression that the store's ideal customer is a nagging, flamboyant Zsa-Zsa Gabor type. Not so. Inside, the boutique is jam-packed with high-end, high-fashion designers for the true Upper East Side woman.

· *Emanuelle Khanh wool suit $1360*

· **Christian Lacroix** · **Claude Montana** · **Emanuel Ungaro**
· **Emmanuelle Khanh** · **Georges Rech** · **Giuliana Teso**
· **Jaques Fath** · **Kenzo** · **Lolita Lempicka** · **Max Chaoul**
· **Nina Ricci** · **Sophie Sitbon** · **Thierry Mugler** · **Jean Yu**

🕐 M-Sat 11-7, Th 11-8, Sun 12-5
Store credit w/in 5 days w/ receipt.

A | B- | A+ |

Precision

1310 Third Ave.   (@ 75th)   212-879-4272

This small boutique is crammed with a limited selection of popular labels, so shoppers can easily hone in on the hottest clothes of the moment: skin-tight pants, button-downs for work, and skirts for cocktail parties.

· *Tark pants $225*

· **3 Dots** · **Earl Jeans** · **Easel** · **Icon** · **James Perse**
· **Juicy Couture** · **Michael Stars** · **Tark** · **Theory** · **Vertigo**

🕐 M-Sat 11-8, Sun 12-6:30
Store credit w/in 7 days w/ receipt.Sale items final.

C+ | B | A- |

Big Drop

1321 Third Ave.   (75th/76th)   212-988-3344

Big Drop carries some up-and-coming designers with big talent, as well as some familiar favorites. A wonderful collection of unique handbags also helps qualify this shop as a worthy destination. **Best Find: Snakeskin purse $225**.

· *Sweater dress $300*

· **6 by Martin Margiela** · **Big Drop** · **Earl Jeans**
· **Juicy Couture** · **Rebecca Dannenberg** · **Tracy Reese**
· **Urchin** · **Vanessa Bruno** · **Wayne Cooper** · **White & Warren**

🕐 M-Sat 11-8, Sun 11-7
Store credit w/in 7 days.

C- | B+ | A- |

Gamine

1322 Third Ave.   (75th/76th)   212-472-6918

For the goddess inside of you, this store offers an ultra-feminine, exotic selection, from short daytime dresses to sexy nighttime numbers. Gamine has a thorough selection of happening dress-up clothes that will appeal to the most frou-frou fantasies. **Best Find: Christiana beaded evening bag $78**.

· *Silky slip dress $248*

· **Christiana** · **Dafna** · **Lotta** · **Lotusa** · **Mary Leong**
· **Vivienne Tam**

🕐 M-Sat 11-8, Sun 12-6
Store credit w/in 7 days.

B+ | A- | A- |

THIRD AVENUE

Pelle Via Roma
1322A Third Ave. (75th/76th) *212-327-3553*

The real versions of these bags, found at boutiques such as Hermès and Tod's, will cost you an arm and a leg. At Pelle Via Roma they will just cost you a hand. The replicas are clever enough to warrant the prices. The only thing these bags lack are the stamp from the original fashion house itself.

· *Tod's copy $500*

· **Pelle Via Roma**

🕐 M-F 10-8, Sat 10-7, Sun 11-6
Exchange w/in 7 days w/ receipt.

    C+ | B+ | A |

Anik
1355 Third Ave. (77th/78th) *212-861-9840*

Anik is like a dream closet filled with all of your favorite middle-range designers. It offers the best pieces from each collection and is ideal for the hip working woman of the new millennium. Wear a suit to work and then whip off the jacket on your way out of the office to reveal the tank underneath.

· *Theory jean jacket $175*

· **Bianca Nero** · **Chaiken & Capone** · **Easel** · **Index**
· **Isabel Ardee** · **Jill Stuart** · **Juicy Couture** · **Kostum**
· **Page 3** · **Susanna Monaco** · **Teen Flo** · **Theory** · **Urchin**
· **Velvet** · **Yigal Azrouel**

🕐 M-Sat 10:45-8, Sun 12-7
Store credit w/in 7 days w/ receipt.

    C+ | B | A- |

Emilio Pucci
24 East 64th St. (5th/Madison) *212-752-4777*

Throughout the years Pucci has featured the same type of brightly colored geometric patterns printed on silky smooth fabrics. To many people, these collectible garments scream "retro," so you might be surprised to learn that Pucci is still going strong. Of course, if you didn't like Pucci designs in the '70s, you aren't going to like them any better now.

· *Silk blouse $1090*

· **Emilio Pucci**

🕐 M-Sat 10-5
Store credit w/in 30 days w/ receipt.

    A- | A- | A |

Delle Celle
17 East 67th St. (5th/Madison) *212-744-5820*

This is a reliable spot for older women whose wardrobe consists primarily of suits, scarves, and more suits. The cuts are conservative and boxy, which is exactly what Delle Celle's customers seem to want.

· *Sportswear jacket $395*

· **Delle Celle**

🕐 M-Sat 10:30-6
Refund w/in 10 days.

    C- | C+ | A- |

service | presentation | quality | expense

Lee Anderson
23 East 67th St. (5th/Madison) 212-772-2463

You might reasonably expect some solicitousness when you're having clothes custom made, but you won't find it here. The Lee Anderson sales people are, shall we say, very selective when choosing which customers will receive their attentions. Their usual client is a wealthy conservative woman who knows her style and isn't about to change it; nor will she tolerate being ignored. If you want service at Lee Anderson, it's best to act like a grande dame.

· *Tafetta skirt and top outfit $2000*

· **Lee Anderson**

☺ M-Sat 11-6
All sales final.

    D+ | **B** | **A** |

Steven Stolman
22 East 72nd St. (5th/Madison) 212-249-5050

If altitude were an indicator of quality, you'd know why this shop is on the fourth floor of its brownstone building. The clothes are fabulous. Stolman produces relatively inexpensive, well-made, and very stylish evening wear. The collection focuses on a few basic pieces in a variety of materials and colors: ballroom skirts, twin sets, pants, and gowns, all of which can be mixed and matched with one another or with something you already own. **Best Find: Silk and tafetta ballroom skirt $325.**

· *Sweater set: cardigan $175, underpiece $125*

· **Steven Stolman**

☺ M-F 10-6, Sat 11-5
Store credit w/in 10 days.

    A- | **A-** | **A** |

Mom's Night Out/One Night Out
147 East 72nd St., 2nd Floor (Lexington/3rd) 212-744-6667

If black-tie galas are a rarity in your life and buying an expensive gown is not in the budget, One Night Out will rent you a designer frock at a very reasonable price. Or if you have a specific dress in mind, the store will custom-make it based on the in-house samples, no matter what your size. Moms-to-be fretting over finding an evening dress to accommodate their bellies can come here too: half the shop specializes in rental and custom maternity evening wear.

· *Silk taffeta gown by Ono $1800*

· **Badgley Mischka · Calvin Klein · Halston · Kay Unger**
· **Mom's Night Out (maternity) · One Night Out · Prada**
· **Vera Wang · Victoria Royal**

☺ MWF 10:30-6, T-Th 10:30-8, Sat 11-5
Store credit w/in 2 weeks.

    A | **A-** | **A** |

service | presentation | quality | expense

EAST 72ND STREET

Jimmy's
150 East 72nd St.   (Lexington/3rd)   212-628-6700

This store is located in a residential building, making it easy to miss. Jimmy's features the most exceptional pieces from all the couture fashion lines, from casual-wear like jeans with transparent sequins to the most formal chiffon gown. The in-house tailor will mold the clothing to your body at no additional cost, and the delightful owners, who treat each customer with the utmost personal attention, make the high prices a bit easier to bear.

· *Suede Roberto Cavalli cap sleeve top $729*

· **Alexander McQueen** · **Anya Hindmark** · **Avon Celli**
· **Chlöe** · **Fendi** · **Jimmy Choo** · **John Galliano**
· **Loro Piana** · **Luciano Barbera** · **Narciso Rodriguez**
· **Pamela Dennis** · **Piazza Sempione** · **Randolph Duke**
· **Richard Tyler** · **Vera Wang**

☺ M-Sat 10-6
Store credit w/ receipt.

A+ | **A** | **A+** |

Midtown

A. Testoni	Kenneth Cole*
A/X Armani Exchange*	Lacoste
Ann Taylor*	Leather Impact
Ann Taylor Loft*	Lederer
Bally	Linda Dresner
Banana Republic*	Louis Féraud
Barami*	Louis Vuitton*
Bebe*	Macy's
Bergdorf Goodman	Manolo Blahnik
Brooks Brothers*	Maraolo*
Burberry	Mikai*
Caché	N. Peal
Celine	The New York Look*
Chanel	Nine West*
Christian Dior	Norma Kamali
Coach*	Otto Tootsi Plohound*
Country Road*	Prada
Daffy's*	Prada (shoes)
Dana Buchman	Precision*
Dollar Bills	Saint Gill
Eileen Fisher*	Saks Fifth Avenue
Eleny	Salvatore Ferragamo
Emporio Armani*	Searle*
Episode	Signature
Express*	St. John
Felissimo	Stuart Weitzman
Fendi	Suarez
Fogal*	The J. Peterman Company
French Connection*	The Original Levi's Store
Gap*	Thomas Pink of Jermyn Street
Geiger	United Colors of Benetton
Gucci	Variazioni
Henri Bendel	Versace
Hermès	Victoria's Secret*
Jennifer Tyler*	Wolford
Jimmy Choo	Workshop

*Additional locations can be found
in the Multiple Store Index pp.152-159.

FIFTH AVENUE

United Colors of Benetton
597 Fifth Ave. (48th/49th) 212-317-2501

Before it was even trendy, Benetton reached the apogee of popularity and name recognition through its politically-correct advertising campaign of the early 80s. Classics on hand include scalloped wool shawls, ribbed scarves and winter duffel coats. Check out the great sales.

· *Thick cotton strap tank with shrug $98*

· **Sisley · United Colors of Benetton**

☺ M-Sat 10-7, Th 10-8, Sun 11-5
Refund w/in 14 days w/ tags and receipts.

C+ | **B** | **B** | **2**

Saks Fifth Avenue
611 Fifth Ave. (@ 50th) 212-753-4000

Once a notoriously snobby department store, Saks is now a hip place where you'll find the most current, stylish and trendy lines. The store is a vertical Madison Avenue, with nine floors and a level for every taste.

· *Michael Kors square-neck knee-length sleeveless dress $295*

Labels include: ABS · Albert Nippon · Anna Sui · Anne Klein · ASAP · Balmain · Carolina Herrera · Dana Buchman · DKNY · Earl Jeans · Eileen Fisher · Ellen Tracy · Emanuel · Gucci · IKCB · Joan Vass · Joseph · Lafayette NY 148 · Laundry · Lilli Pulitzer · Michael Kors · Narciso Rodriguez · Oscar de la Renta · Philippe Adec · Ralph Lauren · Richard Tyler · Shoshanna · Tahari · Vera Wang · Vivienne Tam

☺ M-Sat 10-7, Th 10-8, Sun 12-6
Refund w/ receipt. Store credit otherwise.

C+ | **A-** | **A+** | **4**

Banana Republic
626 Fifth Ave. (@ 50th) 212-974-2350

Once the home of faux safari wear, Banana Republic has evolved over the years into a store that can be summarized in one word: safe. You can hardly go astray, but if you make shopping here a habit, you risk looking awfully plain Jane.

· *Cashmere and wool ankle-length skirt $168*

· **Banana Republic**

☺ M-Sat 9-9, Sun 10-8
Refund w/ receipt. Store credit w/out receipt.

B- | **B+** | **B+** | **2**

A/X Armani Exchange
645 Fifth Ave. (@ 51st) 212-980-3037

The lowest quality level on the Armani totem pole, A/X Armani Exchange attempts to target the younger set by dazzling it with boring basics like jeans and white button-down shirts.

· *Cotton/polyester skirt $78*

· **A/X Armani Exchange**

☺ M-Sat 10-8, Sun 10-7
Refund w/ tags and receipt.
Store credit otherwise.

A- | **C+** | **B+** | **3**

Jimmy Choo
645 Fifth Ave.   (@ 51st)   212-593-0800

Jimmy Choo is to hipsters as Manolo Blahnik is to the Park Avenue set. The exquisite shoes are very expensive, very chic, and very uncomfortable. But if you're willing to suffer for style, head for this cozy boutique, which carries a range of sexy stilettos, knee-high boots, and funky summer slides.

· *Black suede knee-high stiletto boots $785*

· **Jimmy Choo**

☺ M-Sat 10-6
Store credit w/ receipt.

C | B+ | A |

Versace
647 Fifth Ave.   (@ 52nd)   212-317-0224

Versace's Fifth Avenue store is just what you'd expect from the brand that goes beyond mere luxury to outright opulence. The multi-level shop is breathtakingly beautiful, designed to focus maximum attention on every garment. The clothing is obscenely expensive—and sometimes, in the case of the more revealing styles, it's just plain obscene. For well-toned women of means, Versace is the place. **Best Find: Black burnout velvet dress with turquoise shells $3499.**

· *Sequined black pants $1792*

· **Versace**

☺ M-Sat 10-6:30, Sun 12-6
Store credit w/ receipt.

C- | A+ | A+ |

Salvatore Ferragamo
661 Fifth Ave.   (52nd/53rd)   212-759-3822

A destination not just for the mature woman, but also for the younger shopper with a discriminating eye who can see the potential in clothes that might at first seem stuffy. Strikingly patterned scarves can be transformed into sexy halters for evening, and silk-scarf blouses can be teamed with worn-in jeans for a surprising, chic look.

· *Long strap mesh purse $1250*

· **Salvatore Ferragamo**

☺ M-Sat 10-6, Th 10-7
Refund w/in 14 days w/ receipt.

B | A- | A+ |

A. Testoni
665 Fifth Ave.   (52nd/53rd)   212-223-0909

A long-standing favorite of older, well-heeled women, this shoe boutique always produces classic, conservative footwear. Finally hip to the fact that classic doesn't have to be boring, it delivers styles that have been reborn in vibrant colors, like a deep red, and even gets as outrageous as a wild leopard print.

· *Ballet slipper-style flats $235*

· **A. Testoni**

☺ M-F 10-7, Sat 10-6:30, Sun 12-5
Store credit w/in 10 days w/ receipt.

C+ | B- | A |

FIFTH AVENUE

Brooks Brothers
666 Fifth Ave. (52rd/53th) 212-261-9440

The least impressive of New York's three Brooks Brothers, this store carries most of the same classically styled, well-made merchandise that you will find at the other stores, but it lacks their ambiance. Look for cashmere sweaters, twin-sets, straight skirts, pleated slacks, and any other items you might wish to accessorize with a string of pearls. **Best Find: Blue silk v-neck cardigan $88.**

· *Cotton shirt $58*

· **Brooks Brothers**

☺ M-F 10-8, Sat-Sun 10-7
Refund w/in 1 year.

B | **C+** | **A-** |

St. John
665 Fifth Ave. (@ 53rd) 212-755-5252

Those women who want a bit more glam and decadence for their bucks will be drawn to the beaded evening gowns. In this boutique you're buying a name, not a style, and while you can't buy elegance, you can purchase a reputable label.

· *Wool blend evening dress with rhinestones $1098*

· **St. John**

☺ M-F 10-7, Sat 10-6, Sun 11-6
Refund w/in 10 days w/ receipt.

B | **B+** | **A** |

Nine West
675 Fifth Ave. (@ 53rd) 212-319-6893

In its earlier days this line of shoes was inexpensive and poor in quality. Today the prices remain low, but the quality has improved and the styles replicate some of the most popular high-end shoe lines. Nine West makes an exceptional line of knock-offs at prices low enough to qualify it as the Designer Impostor of the footwear world. If you like Prada and Robert Clergerie, you'll love Nine West.

· *Knee-high suede boots $159*

· **Nine West**

☺ M-Sat 10-7, Sun 12-6, Th 10-7:30
Refund w/in 30 days w/ receipt.

C+ | **B+** | **B** |

Christian Dior
703 Fifth Ave. (@ 55th) 212-223-4646

This couture boutique remains a timeless favorite. Filled with elegant suits perfectly tailored to fit the slender socialites who can afford them, Christian Dior maintains the level of refinement it established long ago. The sophisticated clothes are occasionally a bit uptight, but the selection of sleek, chic handbags breaks all age barriers. **Best Find: Blue zebra print pony bag $900.**

· *Bias-cut floral silk dress with spaghetti strap $2750*

· **Christian Dior**

☺ M-Sun 10-6, Th 10-7
Store credit w/ receipt.

B | **B** | **A+** |

Henri Bendel
712 Fifth Ave.   *(55th/56th)*   212-247-1100

Henri Bendel's maze layout requires you to peruse nearly every nook and cranny as you shop the multi-level department store. Women who want an eclectic selection of popular fashions to choose from will be overwhelmed by Bendel's impressive collection.

· *Hot pink leather pedal pushers $328*

Labels include: Anna Molinari · Bajra · Betsey Johnson · Beverly Mehl · Blumarine · Capucine Puerari · Catherine · Champol Serimont · Diane Von Furstenberg · Easel · Elspeth Gibson · Henri Bendel · Isabel Marant · Jean Paul Gaultier · Jemima Khan · Laundry · Margot Razanska · Michael Kors · Nanette Lepore · Nicole Miller · Parosh · Patty Shelabarger · Paul & Joe · Rebecca Taylor · Romeo Gigli · Shoshanna · Stella Cadente · Susan Lazar · Tracy Reese · Vivienne Tam · Whistles

☻ M-Sat 10-7, Th 10-8, Sun 12-6
Refund w/in 30 days w/ receipt.

B | **A** | **A** |

Fendi
720 Fifth Ave.   *(@ 56th)*   212-767-0100

For a while, Fendi was stuck in a rut, appealing mostly to conservative, older women. But thanks to the baguette, Fendi couldn't be more popular or stylish. Young fans of this fashion house will thank their moms who saved those Fendi logo handbags. The clothing line has also undergone a major overhaul, and boasts an impressively hip collection that ranges from pink floor-length shearling coats to stunning gowns.

· *Sequins/beaded hand bag with blue snake strap $1595*

· **Fendi · Fendissime**

☻ M-Sat 10-6, Th 10-7
Store credit w/in 10 days w/ receipt.

A- | **A** | **A+** |

Prada
724 Fifth Ave.   *(56th/57th)*   212-664-0010

Go for the nylon bags. True, you're shelling out $400 on a piece of parachute fabric, but the bags are sleek, classic, oddly elegant, and durable. The Prada symbol will carry you and your bag into the millennium. The Italian loafers are also must-haves and the sweaters in beautiful dark grays and blacks are welcome staples.
Best Find: Olive leather/wool chest bag with fur pocket $590.

· *Orange/green organza and suede zippered vest*

· **Prada · Prada Sport**

☻ M-Sat 10-6, Th 10-7, Sun 12-6
Store credit w/in 6 months w/ receipt.

C | **A** | **A+** | 🐷 4

FIFTH AVENUE

Bergdorf Goodman
754 Fifth Ave.   *(57th/58th)*   212-753-7300

This venerable retail institution has perhaps the most cachet of any of New York's department stores. Bergdorf's caters to sophisticated ladies of the Upper East Side, and carries elite labels, such as Chanel and Chlöe, as well as trendy lines like Theory and Kate Spade. The shoe department justifies un-ironic use of the term "absolutely fabulous." Overall, the finest one-stop shopping in New York. **Best Find: Theory cords $200**.

· *Versace all-metal skirt with fringed mesh and wire-weaved underpinning $7595*

Labels include: Akris · Badgley Mischka · Bergdorf Goodman Collection · Bill Blass · Buccellati · Burberry · Calvin Klein · Celine · Chanel · Chlöe · Dolce & Gabbana · Donna Karan Collection · Escada · Future Ozbek · Giorgio Armani · Hervé Leger · Issey Miyake · John Galliano · Kate Spade · Loro Piana · Luciano Barbera · Mila Schön · Narciso Rodriguez · Pamela Dennis · Ralph Lauren Purple Label · Shin Choi/Coleridge · Strenesse · Theory · Tuleh

☺ M-F 10-7, Th 10-8, Sat 10-6
Refund w/ tags & receipt.

C+ | **A** | **A+** |

Saint Gill
436 Madison Ave.   *(49th/50th)*   212-644-5140

Saint Gill is in the unique position of being the only discount store on the Avenue. Although all of the merchandise is new, the store has the feel of a thrift shop and requires the same keen eye for a find. The junk is hung side-by-side with the gems. **Best Find: Bieff Basix silk chiffon beaded dress $389**.

· *Knit sweater tank $29*

· Bieff Basix · Bill Blass · Ecaille · Enrico Ferezi · George Simonton · Ice Cube · Jackie Jon · Jovani · Marvin Richards · Milia · Nina Ricci · Nolan Miller · Sin

☺ M-Th 10-7, F 10-3, Sun 10-6
All sales final.

B+ | **C-** | **B** |

Lederer
457 Madison Ave.   *(@ 51st)*   212-355-5515

Quality, traditionally-styled handbags are this store's bread and butter. Excluding a seasonal infusion of a few new colors and styles, Lederer carries essentially the same pieces year-round. If you crave consistency rather than a fashion frisson, Lederer is your kind of place.

· *Black leather clutch $389*

· Lederer

☺ M-Sat 9:30-6, Th 9:30-6:30
Store credit w/in 14 days w/ receipt.

B- | **B** | **A** |

Fogal
510 Madison Ave.   (@ 53rd)   *212-355-3254*

Over 80 colors and a variety of patterns of stockings are jammed into this compact Swiss hosiery boutique. If you're already up to your ears in stockings, check out the selection of bodysuits, swimwear and lingerie also offered at Fogal. Prices are a bit steep for hosiery, but you pay for high quality.

· *Cashmere tights $350*

· **Fogal**

☺ M-Sat 10-6:30, Th 10-8
Refund if unopened w/ receipt.

    A- | **C+** | **A+** |

Thomas Pink of Jermyn Street
520 Madison Ave.   (@ 53rd)   *212-838-1928*

Lovers of classic button-down shirts think Pink. The large store with with an Old Money ambiance carries a huge selection of exquisitely-tailored shirts in a variety of colors, from subtle light-pink to bold kelly-green. The shirts can be worn with anything, jeans to suits, though they require cufflinks. Luckily, Pink supplies those too.

· *Crew-neck cashmere sweater $225*

· **Thomas Pink**

☺ M-F 10-7, Th 10-8, Sat-Sun 11-5
Refund w/in 14 days w/ receipt.
Store credit w/out receipt.

    A+ | **A** | **A** |

Lacoste
543 Madison Ave.   (@ 55th)   *212-750-8115*

Everyone knows the alligator icon, and apparently some aren't tired of it yet. An Izod kind of girl will love the T-shirt dresses, but beyond that, you won't find anything too exciting in this ultra-preppy store.

· *White cotton tennis skirt $115*

· **Lacoste**

☺ M-Sat 10-6, Th 10-8, Sun 11-5
Store credit w/ receipt.
Credit to credit card accounts.

    B | **B-** | **B** |

Coach
595 Madison Ave.   (@ 57th)   *212-754-0041*

Coach's new flagship store will delight new customers and amaze old ones. In the past, Coach has made only small, classic, and conservative leather goods. Now, following the lead of Louis Vuitton, Coach has radically updated its image. But never fear: all of the old favorites are still here, along with the python and pony-hair.

· *No-dye leather vinchetta tote $498*

· **Coach**

☺ M-F 10-8, Sat 10-7, Sun 11-6
Refund w/ receipt.
Store credit w/out receipt.

    A | **A-** | **A** |

MADISON AVENUE

Emporio Armani
601 Madison Ave.   *(57th/58th)*   *212-317-0800*

No other designer mixes trendy pieces and timeless elegance like Giorgio Armani. It features everything from streamlined wool pant-suits to transparent body-suits and fringed colorful skirts.

· *Evening suit $800*

· **Emporio Armani**

☺ M-F 10-8, Sat 10-7, Sun 12-6
Store credit w/in 10 days.

A- | B+ | A |

Searle
609 Madison Ave.   *(57th/58th)*   *212-753-9021*

Formerly known for its suits and shearlings, last spring Searle introduced sportswear and twenty other lines of goods. Now carrying some of the hottest new collections, the store is a viable contender in the battle for women's retail affections.

· *Hip-length fitted shearling jacket $1795*

· **Alice & Trixie · Ashley · Beth Bowley · Betsey Johnson**
· **Buzz 18 · Conchi · Cop Copains · Easel · James Perse**
· **Jane Doe · JET · Jules · Leopold · M Collection**
· **Melanie Apple · Melinda Zoller · Nanette Lepore · Only Hearts**
· **Petro Zillia · Pierre Urbach · Plenty · Product Forum**
· **Rebecca Taylor · Searle · Taglia Unica · Tark**
· **Un jour un sac · William B**

☺ M-F 10-7, Sat 10-6, Sun 12-5
Refund w/in 14 days w/ receipt.

B+ | A | A |

Wolford
619 Madison Ave.   *(58th/59th)*   *212-688-4850*

Women who can afford a $3000 dress do not accessorize it with L'eggs. Instead they go to Wolford, the Austrian hosiery company that makes some of the finest and most unusual stockings in the world. For the more conservative, it also make excellent body-stockings and body-suits in fabulous colors.

· *Body-suits $160-$300*

· **Wolford**

☺ M-Sat 10-6
Refund w/in 14 days w/ receipt.

B- | B | A |

Stuart Weitzman
625 Madison Ave.   *(58th/59th)*   *212-750-2555*

Every graduate should invest in two pairs of these shoes to celebrate her entrance into the real world—one pair of classic black leather pumps for work and one pair of sexy, strappy heels for evenings. Women of all ages jockey for space on the cushioned seats in this store, trying on boxfuls of the classic, stylish, well-priced shoes.

· *Patent-leather Mary Janes with heel $195*

· **Stuart Weitzman**

☺ M-F 10-6:30, Sat 10-6, Sun 12-5
Refund w/in 14 days.

C+ | B | A |

service | presentation | quality | expense

Episode
625 Madison Ave.   *(58th/59th)*   *212-755-6061*

There is little that distinguishes Episode from its mid-priced, middle-of-the-road fashion competitors. The selection consists largely of suits, with some sportswear and seasonally appropriate pieces. **Best Find: Ankle-length full skirt with tulle underpinning $360.**

· *Wool blend pinstripe suit, jacket $350, pants $230*

· **Episode** · **Jeselle**

☺ M-F 10-7, Sat 10-6, Sun 12-5
Store credit w/in 10 days w/ receipt.

| A- | | B- | | A- | |

Bally
628 Madison Ave.   *(@ 59th)*   *212-751-9082*

Ideally, to shop at Bally you should be over 30, very well turned out, and extremely well paid. The leather products are simple, well crafted pieces that blend easily into any high-end wardrobe. The store knows what it does best and does not deviate, so don't expect anything designed to catch a trend. **Best Find: Black leather mini-traveler $550.**

· *Black leather hip-length double-breasted jacket $895*

· **Bally**

☺ M-F 10-6:30, Th 10-7, Sat 10-6, Sun 12-5
Refund w/in 30 days w/ receipt. Exchange after 30 days.

| A | | A- | | A | |

Suarez
450 Park Ave.   *(56th/57th)*   *212-753-3758*

Some imitations are so cunning that even women who can afford the real thing buy them. At Suarez, imitations of Kelly bags, Jackie O. bags, and other coveted items fill the store. Compared to the pieces they mimic, the copies are reasonably priced.

· *Turqoise Jackie O. bag $395*

· **Suarez**

☺ M-F 10-6, Sat 10-5
Refund w/in 30 days w/ receipt. Store credit afterwards.

| B+ | | B | | A- | |

Linda Dresner
484 Park Ave.   *(58th/59th)*   *212-308-3177*

The modern aesthetic of Linda Dresner's store design and merchandise is refreshing for Park Avenue. The store features the gamut—jeans to couture evening wear—from a mix of the best European designers, and includes an entire Jil Sander boutique. **Best Find: Chlöe short lace dress $390.**

· *Dries Van Noten velvet fitted blazer with beading $875*

· **Akira** · **Alberta Ferretti** · **Alexander McQueen**
· **Ann Demeulemeester** · **Antonio Berardi** · **Chlöe**
· **Colette Dinnigan** · **Colovos** · **Comme des Garçons** · **Daryl K**
· **Dosa** · **Dries Van Noten** · **Helmut Lang** · **Jil Sander** · **Joan Vass**
· **John Galliano** · **Linda Dresner** · **Marni** · **Narciso Rodriguez**
· **Tracy Feith** · **Veronique Branquinho** · **Wink**

☺ M-Sat 10-6
Refund w/in 7 days w/ receipt.

| B+ | | A | | A+ | |

service | presentation | quality | expense

Geiger
505 Park Ave.   **(@ 59th)**   **212-644-3435**

Geiger carries essentially the same basic line every year, with seasonal updates. All of its coats, suits, and skirts are made of 100% boiled wool, and the classic car coats are available in mother/daughter sizes. **Best Find: Wool ankle-length coat $795.**

· *Print wool wrap-around skirt $382*

· **Geiger**

☺ M-Sat 10-6, Th 10-8
Refund w/in 10 days w/ receipt.

    A | **B+** | **A** |

Signature
686 Lexington Ave.   **(56th/57th)**   **212-644-0505**

Signature is a truly mixed bag of styles and sensibilities. The store's selection of day wear is outshone by its evening wear; you'll find a large selection of provocative black-tie outfits. **Best Find: Juan Carlos Piñera silk halter with crystal beads $230.**

· *Essendi silk spandex long-sleeve T $106*

· **Bette Paige · Blue Birdy · Diab'less · Easel · Enzo Loco · Essendi · Juan Carlos Piñera ·Lili La Agresse ·Lola · Lulu ·Maria Bianca Nero · Motor · Ronen Chen · Sharagano · Tark ·Vertigo**

☺ M-Sat 10-8, Sun 12-6
Store credit w/in 14 days w/ tags & receipt.

    B | **B** | **B+** |

Jennifer Tyler
705 Lexington Ave.   **(@ 57th)**   **212-644-9175**

Jennifer Tyler offers numerous styles and colors in classic cashmere. The sweaters tend to be on the roomy side and the prices are standard for cashmere, so if you're looking for fitted and/or discount items, you'll probably be disappointed. Jennifer Tyler also carries a great selection of cashmere coats and pants. **Best Find: Oversize cashmere and silk cable-knit sweater $425.**

· *Fitted cashmere cardigan with pearl buttons $185*

· **Brunello Lucinelli · Jennifer Tyler · John Lang · Lombarda Lassani**

☺ M-Sat 10-7, Sun 12-6
Store credit w/ receipt. Sale items final.

    C+ | **C+** | **A** |

Precision
522 Third Ave.   **(@ 35th)**   **212-683-8812**

This small boutique is crammed with a limited selection of popular labels, so shoppers can easily hone in on the hottest clothes of the moment: skin-tight pants, button-downs for work, and skirts for cocktail parties. While the sales people are a bit pushy, young locals may find something worth their troubles.

· *Tark pants $225*

· **3 Dots · Earl Jeans · Easel · Icon · James Perse · Juicy Couture · Michael Stars · Tark · Theory · Vertigo**

☺ M-F 11:30-8, Sat 11-8:30, Sun 12-6
Store credit w/in 7 days w/ receipt.
Sale items final.

    C+ | **B** | **A-** |

service | presentation | quality | expense

Caché
805 Third Ave.   *(49th/50th)*   212-588-8719

Caché carries sportswear and suits under its own brand, but dresses are still its specialty. Floor-length beaded gowns that look as if they've come from the wardrobe department of Dynasty and Falcon Crest fill the back of the store. **Best Find: Asymmetrical lycra skirt with lace trim $128.**

· *Satin and lace bustier and ankle-length skirt $325*

· **Caché**

🕑 M-F 10-7, Sat 10-6, Sun 12-6
Refund w/in 14 days w/ receipt. Store credit otherwise.

B- | B- | B+ | 3

Ann Taylor
850 Third Ave.   *(@ 52nd)*   212-308-5333

This is not the boring Ann Taylor of years past. Today the clothes are quite stylish, while remaining classic. If there is one store in the city that caters to women of all ages and body types, Ann Taylor is it.

· *Cotton flat-front pants $48*

· **Ann Taylor**

🕑 M-F 10-8, Sat 10-6, Sun 12-5
Refund w/ receipt. Store credit w/out receipt.

B- | A- | B+ | 2

Macy's
151 West 34th St.   *(7th/Broadway)*   212-695-4400

Macy's offers little you can't get elsewhere. The thrill of revisiting this American institution is tempered by crowds with enough holiday spirit to last even through the off-seasons.

· *Kasper silver shimmer jacket dress $268*

Labels include: ABS · Anna Sui · August Silk · BCBG · Betsy Johnson · Bisou Bisou · Dana Buchman · DKNY · Esprit · French Connection · FUBU · Girbaud · Jones NY · Juicy Couture · Karen Kane · Laundry · Levi's · Linda Allard for Ellen Tracy · Max Studio · Mudd · Necessary Objects · Parallel · Ralph · Rampage · Tadashi · Tahari · Tommy Girl · Tommy Hilfiger · Vivienne Tam · XOXO

🕑 M-Sat 10-8:30, Sun 11-7
Refund w/ receipt. Store credit w/out.

D+ | C- | B+ | 3

Leather Impact
256 West 38th St.   *(7th/8th)*   212-302-2332

This is not a clothing store but rather an impressive collection of leather, suede, and other exotic skins in every color imaginable. A designer favorite, Leather Impact sells all these hides by the yard, so you can take the goods elsewhere and have them transformed into custom designs.

· **N/A**

🕑 M-F 9:30-5:30
All sales final.

B+ | B- | A- | 2

EAST 42ND STREET

Dollar Bills
32 East 42nd St. (5th/Madison) 212-867-0212

If you were whisked inside without noting the tacky name and hadn't yet had a chance to look at the price tags, you'd never guess that you were in a discount store. The high-end clothing is grouped by designer, and the shop boasts a full range of sizes and colors within each line, including Missoni and Byblos.

· *Byblos wool/spandex pant suit $279*

· **N/A**

☺ M-F 8-7, Sat 10-6, Sun 12-5
Refund w/in 7 days. Store credit w/in 14 w/ receipt.

B+ | B- | A |

The J. Peterman Company
107 East 42nd St. (Park/Lexington) 212-370-0855

Although J. Peterman's catalogue pre-dates Seinfeld, Elaine's character certainly raised the store's profile. Now a large boutique, the store carries items purported to be collected from J. Peterman's travels around the world. Some may opt for the Chinatown version of an authentic Asian dress, but the store has a personality worth checking out. **Best Find: Pure silk Indian-style dress $268.**

· *Sheer black silk and lace 1920's-style blouse $138*

· **The J. Peterman Co.**

☺ M-F 8-7, Sat 10-8, Sun 8-6
Refund w/in 60 days w/ tags and receipt.

B+ | B+ | A- |

Ann Taylor Loft
150 East 42nd St. (@ Lexington) 212-885-8766

The unofficial clothier of dress-down Fridays, Ann Taylor Loft is a hybrid of basic work attire and casual weekend wear. The merchandise is practical but bland, ranging from standard tops to casual pants. **Best Find: Wool/spandex-flat front pant $69.**

· *Boat-neck silk sweater $49*

· **Ann Taylor Loft**

☺ M-F 9-9, Sat 10-9, Sun 11-6
Refund w/ receipt. Store credit w/out receipt.

B+ | B | B+ |

Manolo Blahnik
31 West 54th St. (5th/6th) 212-582-3007

Sexy stilettos rule at Manolo Blahnik! Whether your pair came out of the shop last week or fifteen years ago, it's still of-the-moment. Blahnick's signature pointy-toed, needle-thin heels make your legs look as if you've actually put your StairMaster to use, and the huge variety of colors and fabrics makes choosing a real dilemma. Only Manolo Blahnik could make turquoise pony-hair stilettos as versatile as black leather pumps. **Best Find: Blue pony-hair mules $450.**

· *Red pony-hair slingbacks $515*

· **Manolo Blahnik**

☺ M-F 10:30-6, Sat 10:30-5:30
Store credit w/in 60 days.

C+ | A | A+ |

Variazioni
37 West 56th St. (5th/6th) 212-980-4900

Leisurely browsing is an impossibility at this boutique, since the sales people leap on every opportunity to strong-arm you into buying any piece in which you show the vaguest flicker of interest. If you can survive the commission-driven barrage, you will find some very great pieces that run the gamut from a casual cardigan to a formal crepe gown.

· *Lluis wool turtleneck sweater $165*

· **Anna Sui** · **Catherine** · **Claudie Pierlot** · **Easel** · **Laundry**
· **Martine Sitbon** · **Philosophy** · **Rosae Nichols** · **Sonia**
· **Theory** · **Urchin** · **Variazioni** · **Vivienne Tam**

☉ M-Sat 10-7:30, Sun 12-6
Store credit w/in 10 days.

| D | A- | A- | |

Norma Kamali
11 West 56th St. (5th/6th) 212-957-9797

Though the hype for Norma Kamali quieted considerably in the mid-80's, her signature styles remain fantastic and this store is fully stocked with them. The cavernous, multi-level shop features both casual wear and elegant evening dresses. Tucked into one of the store's numerous nooks are Kamali's trademark bathing suits. **Best Find: Bias-cut velvet dress with cowlneck $795.**

· *Black wool poncho $1055*

· **Norma Kamali** · **OMO Kamali**

☉ M-Sat 10-6
Store credit w/in 7 days w/ receipt.

| D | A+ | A | |

Felissimo
10 West 56th St. (5th/6th) 212-247-5656

This magnificent, multi-level store is more of a gift-buyer's delight than a clothing store. However, on the second floor, women can find a small selection of formal shawls that can be used to cover imperfect upper bodies or to spice up a simple black dress. And there are other indulgences: Felissimo carries an impressive selection of luxury bedroom attire, from pashmina robes to silk pajamas.

· *Pashmina robe $875*

· **Felissimo**

☉ M-Sat 10-6, Th 10-8
Store credit w/ receipt.

| C | A+ | A | |

N. Peal
5 West 56th St. (5th/6th) 212-333-3500

There is nothing thrilling about these traditional cashmere sweaters, but they will wear well and the quality is exceptional. The colors of these heartbreakingly soft sweaters are traditional (pastels, conservative darker hues) and so is the roomy cut.

· *Cashmere cardigan $350*

· **N. Peal**

☉ M-Sat 10-6
Store credit anytime.

| C- | B | A+ | |

WEST 56TH STREET

Louis Féraud
3 West 56th St.   (5th/6th)   *212-956-7010*

Playing it safe with classic cuts and fabrics may be unexciting, but it's never a bad choice. Louis Féraud's house line consists predominantly of simple suits and other day wear. The clothes have an older, conservative feel and the price tags will daunt those who aren't rather well-off. However, if you have been fruitlessly seeking that certain essential in black or brown, head here.

· *Black crêpe pant-suit $1085*

· **Louis Féraud**

☺ M-Sat 10-6, Th 10-7
Refund w/in 30 days w/ receipt.

B | B+ | A |

Gucci
10 West 57th St.   (5th/6th)   *212-826-2600*

Hats off to Tom Ford, who transformed the moribund house of Gucci into a label that represents the epitome of modern style. Ford has combined Gucci's signature designs (such as gold-buckled loafers) with his own glam yet clean-lined sensibility. From slinky low-slung velvet pants to super-vixen leathers, this is the most happening line around.

· *Small Jackie O. with Gucci print $498*

· **Gucci**

☺ M-F 10-6:30, Th 10-7, Sat 10-7, Sun 12-6
Refund w/in 10 days w/ receipt.

C | A | A+ |

Eleny
7 West 56th St.   (5th/6th)   *212-245-0001*

The vast space could suit a queen's clothier and dramatically showcases the glamorous evening wear at this custom boutique. You can have an eye-catching formal gown, an unusual wedding dress, or bridesmaids' dresses made just to your liking. The quality, fabrics, and craftsmanship are of the highest quality.

· *Evening gown $3000*

· **Eleny**

☺ M-Sat 10-6 or by appt.
All sales final (will make alterations).

C+| A | A |

Burberry
9 East 57th St.   (5th/Madison)   *212-371-5010*

Burberry's trademark plaid may hide in the linings of its coats or appear boldly as a hat or handbag fabric. For a while this line was very un-hip, but it has come out of the doldrums and is a favorite today of both the young fashion elite and their more conservative older relatives. Though pricey, any purchase from Burberry is a sound investment in an enduring classic

· *Unlined raincoat $475*

· **Burberry**

☺ M-F 9:30-7, Sat 9:30-6, Sun 12-6
Refund w/ receipt. Exchange for sale items.

C+ | B+ | A+ |

service | presentation | quality | expense

The Original Levi's Store
3 East 57th St.   (5th/Madison)   212-838-2188

The blue jeans hardly need mentioning, but Levi's is an enormous store that has all the basics covered. The T-shirts, button-downs, khakis, and jean jackets are sure to last, though we all know that nothing stands the test of time like the 501 Blues.

· *501 Jeans $54*

· **Levi's**

☺ M-Sat 10-8, Sun 11-6
Refund w/ receipt. Store credit w/outut.

| C+ | | B | | B+ | | |

Hermès
11 East 57th St.   (5th/Madison)   212-751-3181

Exquisite, ever-chic, and sickeningly expensive, Hermès has dressed jet-setting women of means from the Duchess of Windsor's day to our own. If you can scrape together the several thousand dollars you'll need for a Kelly bag (named for Princess Grace) or for one of Hermès' other designs, you'll know that you're investing in one of fashion's most undisputed thoroughbreds. But if you don't have a stratospheric budget, opt for a silk scarf.

· *Scarf $275*

· **Hermès**

☺ M-Sat 10-6, Th 10-7
Refund w/ receipt. Store credit otherwise.

| D+ | | A+ | | A+ | | |

Chanel
15 East 57th St.   (5th/Madison)   212-355-5050

The shopping experience at this iconic fashion house is not unlike the shopping scene from "Pretty Woman." Customers are judged by the amount of money they appear to be worth, which puts a damper on enjoying this beautiful boutique. "Big mistake," as Julia Roberts would say. The classic suits and elegant evening wear are geared towards "ladies who lunch," but younger women can exploit them for their hip potential.

· *Suit $3000*

· **Chanel**

☺ M-F 10-6:30, Th & Sat 10-6
Refund w/in 14 days w/ receipt.

| D | | A | | A+ | | |

Victoria's Secret
34 East 57th St.   (Madison/Park)   212-758-5592

Thanks to its gigantic advertising campaign, Victoria's secret is pretty much out. Though the lingerie looks sexy on its busty cover girls, women in the A-range may have trouble finding the right fit. But the selection is incomparable, the quality is decent, and the price is right, especially during the frequent sales.

· *Miracle bra $28, matching thong $14*

· **Victoria's Secret**

☺ M-Sat 10-8, Sun 12-7
Refund w/ receipt. Store credit w/out receipt.

| C+ | | C+ | | B | | |

EAST 57TH STREET

Otto Tootsi Plohound
38 East 57th St.   *(Madison/Park)*   212-231-3199

Tootsi shoes are so distinctive and stylish that they often experience a fashion resurrection after spending several years in the closet. This store draws shoe fetishists of all ages and backgrounds. **Best Find: Miu Miu pink leather Mary Janes $250.**

· *Josephine black boots $178*

- **· Costume National · Duccio Del Duca · Florence Girardier**
- **· Freelance · Giancarlo Paoli · Gianni Bravo · Goffredo Fantini**
- **· Henne · Jean-Michel Cazabat · Josephine · Miu Miu**
- **· Otto Tootsi Plohound · Prada · Voyage · Who's**

☺ M-W 11:30-7:30, Th-F 11-8, Sat 11-7, Sun 12-6
Store credit w/in 10 days w/ receipt.

| B+ | A | A- | 3 |

Prada (shoes)
45 East 57th St.   *(Madison/Park)*   212-308-2332

This location is all about shoes. Unlike the Fifth Avenue flagship store, this space is small and understated, allowing the merchandise to speak for itself. Prices are high, but so is style. If you're ready to splurge on something outrageous—like green or orange patent-leather mules—make Prada your first stop. **Best Find: Silk open-toed mules with sequins and bow $380.**

· *Brown/pink high-heeled loafers with chestnut trimming $470*

- **· Prada**

☺ M-Sat 10-6, Th 10-7
Store credit w/in 10 days w/ receipt.

| B | B+ | A+ | 4 |

Louis Vuitton
49 East 57th St.   *(Madison/Park)*   212-371-6111

The smaller of Louis Vuitton's two Manhattan shops carries only handbags and small leather goods. These expensive classics will never go out of style. Among the preponderance of items featuring the classic LV yellow-on-brown print, there are occasional surprises, such as fun pastel patent leathers. **Best Find: LV print leather make-up box/train case $1980.**

· *Compact zippered wallet with LV print leather $280*

- **· Louis Vuitton**

☺ M-F 10-6, Th 10-7, Sat 10-5:30, Sun 12-5
Refund w/in 15 days w/ receipt. Store credit otherwise.

| C+ | B- | A+ | 4 |

Celine
51 East 57th St.   *(Madison/Park)*   212-486-9700

Michael Kors has successfully transformed this once-boring line into the perfect blend of classic old-school fashion and modern style. Skinny winter wool pants, canvas duffel coats, and thick cashmere sweaters constitute the bulk of the collection. Check out the handbags, which are destined to be the next big thing.

· *Red/black plaid flanel pants $1495*

- **· Celine**

☺ M-Sat 10-6
Refund w/in 7 days w/ receipt.

| B | B+ | A+ | 4 |

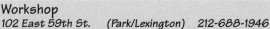

service | presentation | quality | expense

Dana Buchman
65 East 57th St.   (Madison/Park)   212-319-3257

This store carries merchandise for the elegant professional woman who prefers more forgiving styling to the close-fitting clothes of the moment. But even the trendiest young Manhattanite might browse here and find a simple wool sweater, a work suit, or formal dress to suit her taste.

· *Silk-weave tank with turtleneck $198*

· **Dana Buchman**

🕑 M-F 10-7, Sat 10-6, Sun 12-5
Refund w/ receipt w/in 30 days.
Store credit afterward.

  C+ | B+ | A |

Workshop
102 East 59th St.   (Park/Lexington)   212-688-1946

Offering a range of outerwear from basic black jackets to brown and white pony-hair blazers, Workshop has something for every leather fanatic. Most of the shirts, skirts and jackets are made of leather and pony hair, appealing to women who like the security of classical styling mated with the boldness of animal hide. **Best Find: pony-hair brown and white jacket with cow print $1350.**

· *Hip-length, lamb skin, nipped-at-waist coat $825*

· **Workshop**

🕑 M-Sat 10:30-7, Sun 11:30-7
Exchange w/in 21 days.

  B | B | A- |

Chelsea, Flatiron District & Gramercy Park

Agnès B. *
Ann Taylor*
Anthropologie*
Banana Republic*
Barami*
Bebe*
Club Monaco*
Collezioni
Country Road*
Daffy's*
Darrow Vintage Clothing
Eileen Fisher*
Emporio Armani*
Express*
Galleria
Gap*
Intermix*
J. Crew*

Jeffrey
Joan & David*
Jonik
Juno*
Kenneth Cole*
La Galleria La Rue*
Loehman's
Nine West*
Noir et Blanc
Old Navy*
Otto Tootsi Plohound
Rève
Sacco
Sybele
The Original Leather Store*
Victoria's Secret*
Zara

*Additional locations can be found
in the Multiple Store Index pp. 152-159.

SEVENTH AVENUE

Loehman's
101 Seventh Ave.   *(16th/17th)*   *212-352-0856*

Loehman's is famed as the place where high-end discount shopping began, and it still lives up to its decades-old reputation as the home of great finds and fiercely competitive shopping. The store carries three floors of discounted designer clothes, from Katayone Adeli to Calvin Klein. The merchandise is well organized (and labeled) according to designer, and the bargains will simply blow you away—as might some fellow shopper who wants to get her hands on the size-8 black Armani suit that you've just plucked off the rack.

· *Katayone Adeli khakis $39*

Labels include: August Silk · BCBG · Cynthia Steffe · Dana Buchman · Dolce & Gabbana · Donna Karan · Free People · French Connection · Giorgio Armani · Gruppo Americano · Harris Wallace · Isabel Ardee · Jenne Maag · Joseph Abboud · Kasper · Katayone Adeli · Kay Unger · Lafayette NY 148 · Laundry · M-A-G · Max Studio · Nicole Miller · Oliver Yates · Oscar · Parasuco · Polo Sport · Ralph Lauren · Rampage · Romeo Gigli · Soda Blu · Tahari · Theory · Valentino · XOXO

⏱ M-Sat 9-9, Sun 11-7
Refund w/in 14 days w/ receipt.
Store credit otherwise.

D	C+	B+	2

Daffy's
1311 Broadway   *(@ 34th)*   *212-736-4477*

For a designer discount store, Daffy's does a good job of counter-balancing the clutter with high ceilings and clearly delineated departments. A Daffy's shopping experience requires effort and stamina, but there are clear rewards.

· *Equipment silk blouse with velvet overlay $20 (reg. $180)*

· **N/A**

⏱ M-F 10-9, Sat 10-8, Sun 11-7
Refund w/in 14 days w/ receipt.

D	D+	B	2

Burlington Coat Factory
707 Sixth Ave.   *(22nd/23rd)*   *212-229-1300*

Burlington's slogan may be "More than great coats" but the great coats are still the main attraction. While the decor leaves something to be desired and the organization of the merchandise isn't particularly intelligible, you'll find an unparalleled selection of discount outerwear, ranging from classic pea coats to fur-collared dress coats.

· *CK mid-length wool coat $250*

· **ABS · Albert Nippon · Anne Klein · BCBG · Bisou Bisou · Calvin Klein · Evan-Picone · French Connection · Halston · Hervé Benard · Infinity · John Weitz · Jones New York · Kasper · Larry Levine · Liz Claiborne · Marvin Richards · Oleg Cassini · Paloma Picasso · Perry Ellis · Tahari**

⏱ M-F 8-7, Sat 10-6, Sun 11-5
Store credit w/in 14 days w/ receipt.

C-	D+	B+	2

Old Navy
610 Sixth Ave.   *(@ 18th)*   *212-645-0663*

This is the hipper, cooler, younger—and, very key—less expensive version of its parent company, The Gap. The clothes will most appeal to pre-teens and teeny-boppers, but women seeking a good selection of stylish basics may discover a new best friend in Old Navy.

· *Cords $30*

· **Old Navy**

☺ M-Sat 9:30-9:30, Sun 11-8
Refund w/in 30 days w/ receipt. Store credit otherwise.

| C | | C+ | | B- | |

Collezioni
79 Fifth Ave.   *(15th/16th)*   *212-206-1400*

Collezioni carries last year's clothing at discounted prices. If you're not a stickler for trends, you can find great work suits, casual wear, and a limited selection of evening wear at very reasonable prices.

· *Laundry strapless nylon evening dress $198*

· **ABS · BCBG · Bette Paige · Big Star · Bisou Bisou**
· **Calvin Klein · Cheap Thrill · CK Calvin Klein · Côte à Côte**
· **Easel · Erez · Follies · Free People · Jane Doe**
· **Laundry · MLC · Sin · Style · Sweet Romeo · Tahari · THS**

☺ M-Sat 10-8, Sun 12-7:30
Store credit w/in 10 days.

| C | | C | | B- | |

Joan & David
104 Fifth Ave.   *(15th/16th)*   *212-627-1780*

This simple and conservative boutique is known primarily for its shoes, which are trend-conscious without being trendy. The coats and suits lean towards the traditional both in color and cut. Basics that would elsewhere be boring here become elegant essentials, thanks to the fine quality of the merchandise.

· *Silver snakeskin shoes $240*

· **Joan & David**

☺ M-Sat 11-7, Sun 1-6
Refund w/in 10 days. Sale items final.

| B+ | | B | | A | |

Anthropologie
85 Fifth Ave.   *(@ 16th)*   *212-627-5885*

Anthropologie combines popular styles with ethnically-inspired prints and fabrics. Look for the store's fantastic collection of home furnishings, organized according to the country whose traditions inspired them or from which they were imported. **Best Find: Kerri Kahn pony-hair and red leather belt $80.**

· *Corduroy skirt $78*

· **ABS · Anthropologie · Buffalo · Co-op · Curiositees · Double A**
· **Easel · F.r.e.e. · Free People · Hype · Illia · In the Know**
· **Leopold · Liquid · Lulu Lamé · Maxou · Michael Stars**
· **Mini by X-Large · New York Based · Only Hearts · Phillip Chi**
· **Plenty · Sanctuary · Sweat Pea · Sweet Romeo · Tease Tees**
· **Tracy Reese · Work Order**

☺ M-Sat 10-8, Sun 10-5
Refund w/ receipt. Store credit w/out receipt.

| C+ | | A | | B | |

service | presentation | quality | expense

Emporio Armani
110 Fifth Ave.   *(@ 16th)*   *212-727-3240*

No other designer mixes trendy pieces and timeless elegance like Giorgio Armani. This is perhaps truest in his mid-level collection, Emporio Armani, which bridges the gap between the sporty A/X line and the couture line. Featuring everything from streamlined wool pant-suits to transparent body-suits and fringed colorful skirts, Emporio dresses the woman of substance and style.

· *Sheer beeded spaghetti strap body suit $495*
· **Emporio Armani**

🕐 M-F 11-8, Sat 11-7, Sun 12-6
Refund w/in 10 days w/ receipt.

C	A	A	

Kenneth Cole
95 Fifth Ave.   *(@ 17th)*   *212-675-2550*

Kenneth Cole really understands women's casual footwear needs. His shoes strike a balance between current trends and classic style. The result: pony-hair Mary Janes with chunky heels; patent-leather loafers; and wedge-heeled boots. Cole also makes a great collection of bags. Best of all, everything is reasonably priced.

· *Wool wedges $149*
· **Kenneth Cole**

🕐 M-Sat 10-9, Sun 11-7
Refund (w/credit card) or store credit
(w/cash) w/in 21 days w/ receipt.

B+	B+	B+	

Zara
101 Fifth Ave.   *(17th/18th)*   *212-741-0555*

Spain's answer to the Gap, Manhattan's answer to fabulous clothing at great prices. Zara has an enormous selection of stylish high-fashion knock-offs that can always be counted on. The clothes aren't made well and might not survive until next year; but you won't be devastated when you remember how little they cost.

· *Red felt pants $79*
· **Zara**

🕐 M-Sat 10-8, Sun 12-7
Refund w/in 30 days w/ tags.

C	A	B-	

Gap
122 Fifth Ave.   *(17th/18th)*   *212-989-0550*

You can always count on this great American store for staple wardrobe items. The Gap has jumped on the color bandwagon, and throughout the year, cotton shirts in a variety of cuts and colors are available in a variety of spectrums, as are timeless button-downs, great sweats, and wonderful fitted jeans.

· *T-shirts $18*
· **Gap**

🕐 M-F 10-9, Sat 10-8, Sun 11-7
Refund w/ receipt anytime. Store credit w/out receipt.

B-	B+	B	

service | presentation | quality | expense

Barami
119 Fifth Ave.   *(@ 19th)*   **212-529-2300**

Barami offers a cheaper and more work-geared selection of clothing for women of all ages. Barami is no fashion Mecca, but those in need of classic, affordable suits for everyday wear will find a good selection here.

· *Suit - jacket $199, pants $109*

· **Barami**

☺ M-Sun 8-8
Refund w/in 14 days.
Store credit afterwards.

    C+ | **C** | **C** | **2**

Intermix
125 Fifth Ave.   *(19th/20th)*   **212-533-9720**

Intermix has successfully taken the best of the downtown trend-setters and brought them north to this chic shopping spot. The merchandise is a mix of all the newest young designers with some of the best of the established favorites. The handbag selection is truly impressive: half the selection is of the moment, half of the moment yet to come.

· *Vivienne Tam sequined sleeveless dress $498*

· **Alberta Ferretti · Amy Chan · Anna Sui · Catherine**
· **Chaiken & Capone · D&G · Daryl K · Earl Jeans**
· **Helmut Lang · Intermix · Jamin Puech · John Bartlett**
· **Joseph · Katayone Adeli · Kate Spade · Nikki B**
· **Paul & Joe · Plein Sud · Raffe · Rebecca Dannenberg**
· **Rebecca Taylor · Siegerson Morrison · Stella Pace**
· **Theory · Tocca · Tracy Feith · Vivienne Tam**
· **Vivienne Westwood · William B**

☺ M-Sat 11-8, Sun 12-6
Store credit w/in 10 days w/ receipt.
Sale items final.

    C | **B+** | **A-** | **3**

Otto Tootsi Plohound
137 Fifth Ave.   *(20th/21st)*   **212-460-8650**

Tootsi shoes are so distinctive and stylish that they often experience a fashion resurrection. You put them in the back of your closet for a year or two, then discover that they're in style again. There is no such thing as a typical customer in this store, which draws shoe fetishists of all ages and backgrounds. Go: you're sure to find something you like.

· *Heeled ballet slipper $128*

· **Costume National · Duccio Del Duca · Florence Girardier**
· **Freelance · Giancarlo Paoli · Gianni Bravo**
· **Goffredo Fantini · Henne · Jean-Michel Cazabat · Josephine**
· **Miu Miu · Otto Tootsi Plohound · Prada · Voyage · Who's**

☺ M-F 11:30-7:30, Sat 11-8, Sun 12-7
Exchange w/in 10 days w/ receipt.
Sale items final.

    C+ | **A** | **A-** | **3**

FIFTH AVENUE

Jonik
168 Fifth Ave.   *(21st/22nd)*   212-229-9404

Jonik is appropriate for post-teens according to every measure: price, quality, and style. The fashion is what's happening without being too adventurous, and the merchandise doesn't look cheap.

· *Hooded mid-length zippered coat by View $220*

· **2026** · **Annie B.** · **Bhatti** · **Blue Birdy** · **Casting** · **LM Lulu** · **Long Paige** · **Morgan de Toi** · **Ronen Chen** · **View** · **Visage** · **Y London**

☺ M-Th 10-8, F 10-7, Sun 11-5
Store credit w/ receipt.

B- | B- | B |

Juno
170 Fifth Ave.   *(@ 22nd)*   212-647-9064

With several brands, Juno carries a wide selection of trendy footwear. Fashion slaves will be happy to know that they're investing in durable shoes—even if they won't be wearing them next year. **Best Find: Juno pony-hair ankle-length boot with leather laces $187**.

· *Juno Mary Jane with pony strap $185*

· **Debut** · **Everyone** · **Exe** · **Jo Ghost** · **Juno** · **L'Autre Chose** · **Roberto de Carlo** · **Trussardo** · **Vic Matie** · **Zaza**

☺ M-Sat 10:30-8, Sun 12-7
Store credit w/in 7 days w/ receipt.

C+ | B+ | A- |

Galleria
315 Fifth Ave., 2nd Floor   *(@ 32nd)*   212-682-3927

Located on the second floor of an office building, Galleria is difficult to find. Fendi logo bags and Gucci sunglasses are standard fare. An abundant selection of Italian and Korean jeans, for extra-long and skinny legs, would make this a pleasurable shopping experience were it not for the below-par staff.

· *Small Prada make-up bag $95*

· **Byblos** · **Celine** · **Fendi** · **Fendi** · **Gucci** · **MCM** · **Mook Design** · **Perlina** · **Prada** · **Versace**

☺ M-Sun 10-8
Exchange w/in 7 days w/ tags & receipt.

D | C | B+ |

Sybele
432 Third Ave.   *(@ 30th)*   212-213-3999

The store offers one-stop shopping for everything from casual work wear to frilly wrap-dresses to sexy night wear for slim bodies. The staff is incredibly sweet, so Sybele is a fun place to spend a Saturday afternoon trying on clothes with girlfriends.

· *Friponne black straight leg pant $136*

· **2026** · **525** · **Alex(e)** · **Blue Birdy** · **Diane Von Furstenberg** · **Free Follies** · **Friponne** · **Jane Doe** · **Lotta** · **Lulu Paris** · **Mandalay** · **Melda Rossi** · **Michael Stars** · **Michael Stephen** · **Morgan de Toi** · **Rossodisera** · **Sharagano** · **Shoshanna** · **Trina Turk** · **Urchin** · **Yigal Azrouel**

☺ M-Th 11-8, F-Sat 11-7, Sun 12-6
Store credit w/in 5 days w/ receipt.

A- | B | A- |

CHELSEA, FLATIRON AND GRAMERCY

Jeffrey
449 West 14th St.   *(9th/10th)*   *212-206-1272*

Is Barneys missing a floor? Located in the heart of the meat-packing district, Jeffrey is a dead-ringer for Barneys' sixth floor, offering the edgiest too-cool fashions in New York. While much of the clothing is stuff that only a stylist could love, the phenomenal shoe and bag selection will delight everyone—everyone, that is, who can afford to drop hundreds of dollars on a maribou cuff, or some similar to-die-for trifle.

· *Gucci Jackie O. bag $570*

- **Alessandro Dell'Acqua · Alexander McQueen**
- **Ann Demeulemeester · Balenciaga · Balmain**
- **Christian Dior · Clements Ribeiro · Costume National**
- **Dries Van Noten · Fendi · Galliano · Gucci · Helmut Lang**
- **Jean Paul Gaultier · Jil Sander · Katayone Adeli · Kiton**
- **Marni · Michael Kors · Rick Owens · Thimister**
- **Tuleh Courreges**

☺ M-Sat 10-8, Th 10-9, Sun 12-6
Refund w/in 14 days w/ receipt.
Store credit otherwise.

   C+ | A | A |

Express
130 Fifth Ave.   *(@ 18th)*   *212-633-9414*

Express manufactures lesser- quality, lower-priced versions of the most current fashions. The chain is ideal for teenagers but has mass appeal. Whether choosing a T-shirt or a long formal skirt, shoppers should stick to solid colors and simple cuts: when Express gets expressive, the result is usually a tacky disaster. **Best Find: Orange cargo pants with olive trim $45.**

· *Stretchy flat-front micro-twill pants $45*

- **Express**

☺ M-F 10-8, Sat-Sun 12-6
Refund anytime w/ receipt.
Refund at current price w/out receipt.

   C- | B- | B- |

Agnès B.
13 East 16th St.   *(5th/Union Sq. West)*   *212-741-2585*

Agnès B. has captured simple Parisian style and brought it effortlessly to New York. Truly appropriate for a woman of any age, the store is always stylish without being "fashionable." Agnès B. basics have looked the same for over 15 years and they still mix into a woman's wardrobe as if they were conceived of yesterday. **Best Find: Cotton shell hooded coat with fleece lining $600.**

· *Fitted v-neck cotton cardigan $86*

- **Agnès B.**

☺ M-F 11-7, Th 11-8, Sat 11-7, Sun 12-6
Store credit w/in 10 days.

   B | A- | B- | 3

WEST NINETEENTH STREET

Darrow Vintage Clothing
7 West 19th St.   (5th/6th)   212-255-1550

Loud retro music adds to the sensation that you're in a time warp as you peruse racks of vintage clothing. Though you can find some casual attire here, Darrow's strength is in vintage evening and formal wear such as frilly dresses in silk chiffon, lace, and satin. **Best Find: Green lace dress with cap sleeves from early 1930s $250.**

· *Green chiffon dress with sequins $148*

· **N/A**

☉ M-Sat 11-7
Exchange w/in 7 days w/ receipt.

A	B-	B+	2

Noir et Blanc
19 West 23rd St.   (5th/6th)   212-627-1750

The store's owner and sometimes designer has an amazing eye for finding the right pieces for her customers, and best of all, she takes her talents beyond the confines of her store. She'll actually go to your home and tell you what articles of clothing you need to fill out your wardrobe.

· *Teen Flo long wool blazer $360*

· **3 Dots · Anni Kuan · Autumn Cashmere · Beth Bowley · Big Star · Ghost · Irena Gregory · Jenne Maag · Only Hearts · Petit Bateau · Sara Sturgeon · Teen Flo · Time Is · Transit**

☉ M-F 10-7, Th 10-8, Sat 11-6
Store credit w/in 10 days w/ tags and receipt. Sale items final.

A	B-	B+	3

La Galleria La Rue
12 West 23rd St.   (5th/6th)   212-807-1708

La Galleria La Rue mixes everything that's hot in a kaleidoscope of colors and cultures. This French store specializes in outrageous pieces in materials such as leopard, lace, snakeskin, and silk. **Best Find: Faux snakeskin pants $299.**

· *Long black gathered chiffon dress with red slip $375*

· **La Galleria La Rue**

☉ M-Th 12-8, F 12-9, Sat 11-7, Sun 12-6
Store credit w/in 7 days w/ receipt. Sales final on sale items.

C+	B	A-	3

Rève
12 East 23rd St.   (Broadway/Park)   212-529-7626

At first glance Rève might appear tacky, but look again. This store carries anything you might need for an after-eight event, from white-tie ball gowns to black mini-skirts.

· *Badgley Mischka floor-length gown $875*

· **Anti-Flirt · Badgley Mischka · BCBG · Betsey Johnson · Diab'less · Erez · Free Follies · Friponne · Helen Wang · Jill Stuart · Just in Time · Kay Unger · Krizia · Lulu Paris · Morgan de Toi · One Love · Sharagano · Single · Vivienne Tam**

☉ M-Sat 10-8, Sun 12-6
Store credit w/in 7 days.

B	B-	A	3

West Village

Arleen Bowman
Bleecker Leather
Dorothy's Closet
Jungle Planet
La Galleria La Rue
Mieko Mintz
Old Japan
Sleek on Bleecker
Star Struck
The Original Leather Store*
Tibet Kailash
Tibet Treasures
Verve
Village Tannery
Whiskey Dust

*Additional locations can be found
in the Multiple Store Index pp. 152-159.

HUDSON STREET

Whiskey Dust
526 Hudson St.   (W. 10th/Charles)   212-691-5576

Not everything in this impressive collection of authentic western and Native American apparel and accessories has its price. Some of the best pieces can only be rented. But there's plenty to choose from, and what's there is the real McCoy.

· *Suede fringe jacket $525*

· **Chisolm Boots · Ely & Walker · True Grit · Wrangler**

🕑 M-Sat 12:30-7, Sun 1-6
Store credit w/ tags.

C+ | B+ | B- | 3

Star Struck
47 Greenwich Ave.   (Charles/Perry)   212-691-5357

For a vintage clothing store, this place is impressively well-organized. Each clothing type is clearly separated, though most of what you'll find is standard 70s. To spike your Saturday Night Fever you'll find bell-bottoms and button-down shirts, and don't forget to browse the T-shirts for a fun trip down memory lane.

· *Beaded 1950s sweater with hook & eye closures $55*

· **N/A**

🕑 M-Sat 11-8, Sun 12-7
Exchange w/in 7 days.

B- | B | B- | 1

Tibet Kailash
48 Greenwich Ave.   (Charles/Perry)   212-255-9572

This amazing boutique should survive long after the vogue for all things Tibetan has passed. Tibet Kailash brings to downtown New York gorgeous shirts, skirts and dresses that were once available only on the roof of the world. Floor-length skirts and dresses in raw silk come in more than ten shades and have back-tie closures to ensure that one size really does fit all.

· *Silk embroidered Tibetan dress $75*

· **N/A**

🕑 M-Sun 11-9
Exchange w/in 7 days.

B | A | A- | 2

Mieko Mintz
49 Grove St.   (Bleecker/7th)   212-627-1524

Named for the charming designer whose clothes fill the store, Mieko Mintz carries global fare with flair. Each original hand-made piece ingeniously blends Eastern and Western styles. One of Mieko's extraordinary coats—such as the silk kimono shell with mohair collar and lining—might run you $700-$1500. If you don't find anything that suits you, Mieko will design something that does.

· *Hand-made original coats $700-$1500*

· **Amanda Gray · Cut Loose · Kashi · Mieko Mintz · Mike & Todd · Sacred Threads · Sheen**

🕑 M-Sun 1-8
Refund w/in 10 days w/ receipt.

B+ | B- | A- | 3

service | presentation | quality | expense

W E S T   V I L L A G E

La Galleria La Rue
385 Bleecker St.   (@ Perry)   212-352-0961

La Galleria La Rue mixes everything that's hot in a kaleidoscope of colors and cultures. This French store specializes in outrageous pieces in materials such as leopard, lace, snakeskin, and silk. **Best Find: Faux snakeskin pants $299**.

· *Embroidered black satin floor-length skirt $475*

· **La Galleria La Rue**

☺ M-Th 12-8, F 12-9, Sat 11-7, Sun 12-6
Exchange w/in 7 days.

B	A-	A-	

Old Japan
382 Bleecker St.   (Charles/Perry)   212-633-0922

If "Memoirs of a Geisha" has you enraptured, seek out Old Japan. The beautiful and reasonably priced kimonos come in both cotton and silk. They can be worn either as inner- or outerwear or hung decoratively on the wall. The store also offers an exquisite collection of antique furniture and sewing boxes that double as jewelry boxes.

· *Silk hand-painted kimono $100*

· **N/A**

☺ M-Sun 2-7:30
All sales final.

A-	B	A-	

Sleek on Bleecker
361 Bleecker St.   (W. 10th/Charles)   212-243-0284

One of the few homes of contemporary labels in the West Village, Sleek on Bleeker has all the great names, but somehow still lacks punch. The store has collected the cleanest and simplest pieces from each designer, resulting in a sleek—but rather dull—display.

· *Paul & Joe turtleneck sweater with drawstring collar $246*

· **Biscote · Cashmere Studio · Chaiken & Capone**
· **Cynthia Rowley · Daryl K · Easel · Madison Brown**
· **Paul & Joe · Rebecca Dannenberg · Spooner · Theory**
· **Tibi Hyland · Urchin**

☺ M-Sat 12-7:30, Sun 12-6
Exchange w/in 10 days w/ receipt.

B-	B+	A-	

Verve
353 Bleecker St.   (W. 10th/Charles)   212-691-6516

Verve provides a good mix of sophisticated, stylish small- and medium-size day and evening bags. Many lesser-known designers are carried here, so chances are that if you buy a bag, you won't see it on every other arm within the week.

· *Leyla red snake-skin flat shoulder bag $168*

· **Adrienne Vittadini · Carla Mancini · Das · Dollar Grand**
· **Isabella Fiore · Kazuyo Nakano · Leyla · Noir NYC · TTMX**

☺ M-Sat 11-7:45, Sun 12-6
Exchange w/in 7 days.

B+	B+	A	

BLEECKER STREET

Arleen Bowman
353 Bleecker St.   (W. 10th/Charles)   212-645-8740

A cross between West Village hip and Latin-American homespun, Arlene Bowman is an ideal store for bohemian women who prefer comfort and simplicity to the madness of current trends. The collection of clothing is more conscious of fabric than cut and offers many amorphous pieces including knit sweaters and loose-fitting print dresses.

· *Corduroy shirts $75*

· **3 Dots** · **Alex Garfield** · **Arlene Bowman** · **Autumn Cashmere** · **Blue Dragon** · **Chin Chin** · **Claudette** · **Crispina Designs** · **D.A.R.** · **Elaris** · **Flax** · **Hot Knots** · **Hot Socks** · **Johnny Was** · **Lilith** · **Margaret M.** · **Margaret O'Leary** · **Marrika Nakk** · **Nothing Matches** · **Sanctuary** · **Taryn de Chellis**

☺ M-Sat 12-7, Sun 1-6
Exchange w/in 7 days w/ receipt.

A		B+		B+	

Dorothy's Closet
335 Bleecker St.   (Christopher/W. 10th) 212-206-6414

The prices are in the single-digits for 90% of the items (including faux-fur jackets) in this small vintage shop. The quality is understandably mixed, but the prices are so low you wouldn't feel guilty discarding your duds after one wearing only.

· *Seafoam wool peacoat $10*

· **N/A**

☺ M-Sat 11-7, Sun 12-6
Cash only. No refund or exchange.

B		C		C+	

Bleecker Leather
177 Bleecker St. (MacDougal/Sullivan) 212-254-5807

Save your pennies in winter so you can stock up on leather basics during this store's terrific summer sales. The help is happy to assist you in selecting something just right for your needs from the wide selection of leather basics that includes backpacks and briefcases. For price and style, though, the jackets are the main attraction.

· *Leather jacket $350*

· **American Base** · **Oakwood**

☺ M-Th 12-10:30, F 12-1, Sun 12:30-11
Store credit w/ receipt, coats w/in 30 days, shoes 3 months.

A-		A-		A	

Village Tannery
173 Bleecker St. (MacDougal/Sullivan) 212-673-5444

Some stores stand the test of time not because they keep up with the times but because they do not. Twenty-six year-old Village Tannery is one such store. Its goods, such as backpacks and briefcases, are well-constructed and classic.

· *Leather backpack $139*

· **Village Tannery**

☺ M-Th 11-11, F-Sat 11-1am, Sun 11-11
Store credit w/ receipt.

B-		C+		B+	

Jungle Planet
175 West 4th St.   *(6th/7th)*   *212-989-5447*

If you're heading for the tropics, make a pit stop at Jungle Planet. Everything in this store—especially the printed collection of sarongs and hand-painted sandals—is brightly colored and perfect for beachwear in foreign climes.

· *Knit sleeveless turtleneck $58*

· **Bouncy Wear** · **Jungle Planet** · **K2** · **Sergio Valente** · **Transcend**

☺ Sun-Th 12-8, F 12-9, Sat 12-10
Exchange w/in 7 days.

    A- | **B-** | **B** |

The Original Leather Store
171 West 4th St.   *(6th/Jones)*   *212-675-2303*

This West Village boutique sells the gamut of leather goods, from hot pants to cool jackets. Unlike many other leather stores, this store actually cuts its clothing for a woman's frame and makes beautiful body-conscious pieces. And also unlike many other leather stores, the styles here don't appear to be languishing in the mid-80s. **Best Find: Worn-in red leather calf-skin pants $389**.

· *Knee-length lambskin coat $975*

· **Original Leather**

☺ M-W 11-9, Th-Sat 11-12, Sun 12-9
Store credit w/in 45 days.

    B | **B+** | **A-** |

Tibet Treasures
19 Christopher St.   *(Gay/Waverly)*   *646-486-4064*

Tibet Treasures leans farther toward a fashionable aesthetic than some of the other Tibetan stores that have been cropping up downtown of late. It carries the usual fare of pashmina shawls and Tibetan-style cotton shirts, but in unusually beautiful colors. The store also has floor-length raw silk skirts in 25 amazing hues—enough to tempt even those who worship at the shrine of black pants.

· *Raw silk ankle-length skirts $135*

· **N/A**

☺ M-Sun 11-8
Store credit w/ receipt.

    C+ | **B** | **B+** |

Greenwich Village & Noho

Andy's Chee-Pees
Antique Boutique
Atrium
Banana Republic*
Basic Basic
Bond 07 by Selima
Daryl K*
EMS
French Connection*
Gap*
Ibiza
JD
Katayone Adeli
Know Style
La Petite Coquette
Leather Master
Metro
Mikai*
Patricia Fields
Petit Peton
Purdy Girl*
Spooly D's
The Stella Dallas Look
Tibet Arts & Crafts
Untitled
Urban Outfitters*
Veronica Bond
Vision of Tibet

*Additional locations can be found
in the Multiple Store Index pp. 152-159.

SULLIVAN STREET

Veronica Bond
171 Sullivan St.   (Houston/Bleecker)   212-254-5676

Pretty young creatures of the night can find sleek dresses at reason-able prices at Veronica Bond. Though the quality isn't top-notch, the styles are sophisticated. Look for sexy halter-tops, bias-cut spaghetti-strap dresses, and fitted knee-length skirts.

· *Silver sequined top $145*

· **Veronica Bond**

☺ M-Sun 2-7
Exchange w/in 10 days w/ receipt.

| **B-** | | **B-** | | **B-** | |

Vision of Tibet
167 Thompson St.   (Houston/Bleecker)   212-995-9276

Which came first—the pashmina craze or the inundation of down-town Manhattan with Tibetan stores? Twelve-year-old Vision of Tibet transcends this chicken-and-egg conundrum; the store was here long before pashminas draped every uptown arm, and it remains serenely un-trendy. You'll find a rainbow of silk scarves, but the saris are definitely the stand-out item. Though they are meant to be wrapped around the body, you can't help imagining them as a bedspread or tablecloth

· *Hand-made silk sari $390*

· **N/A**

☺ M-Sun 11-7
Exchange w/ receipt.

| **B+** | | **B** | | **B** | |

The Stella Dallas Look
218 Thompson St.   (Bleecker/3rd)   212-674-0447

This thrift store, though small and unassuming, has loads of vintage clothing to pick through. The Stella Dallas Look focuses on girlish dresses, decorative cardigans, and trimmed jackets that look best on young hipsters going for the retro look.

· *Dresses $40-$60*

· **N/A**

☺ Sun-T 4-8, W-Sat 1-8
All sales final.

| **C+** | | **C+** | | **B-** | |

Purdy Girl
220 Thompson St.   (Bleecker/3rd)   212-529-8385

The more casual Purdy Girl sells of-the-moment fashions for less formal occasions. Lucky women who are able to dress casually at work can find reasonably priced pants, skirts and sweaters, as well as cocktail dresses and ponchos, at this location. On the way to the register check out the colorful, trendy accessories such as rhinestone hair pins and crystal bracelets.

· *Silk bandanna-print spaghetti-strap dress by Plenty $142*

· **Co-op · Cristiana · Geisha · Jane Doe · Karibou Silver · Liz Palacios · Pierre Urbach · Plenty · Tessuto · Urchin · Vickie Lee · Vitraux**

☺ Sun-W 11-10, Th-Sat 11-12
Store credit w/in 7 days w/ receipt.

| **B-** | | **B-** | | **B-** | |

GREENWICH VILLAGE AND NOHO

Metro
534 LaGuardia Pl. (Bleecker/3rd) 212-529-4948

Anyone on a shoe-string budget can buy an outfit here without breaking the bank. Filled with inexpensive, super-trendy clothing such as faux-fur leopard print wraps and feather boas, Metro offers inexpensive fashion for the ultimate urbanite.

· *Shearling boa $55*

· **Cheap Thrill** · **Co-op** · **Dollhouse** · **Free Country** · **Free People**
· **Kat Man Doo** · **Luscious** · **NM70** · **Tag Rag** · **Todd Oldham**

☺ Sun-Th 10-10, F-Sat 10-12
Store credit w/in 7 days w/ receipt.

C+		C+		C+	

Purdy Girl
540 LaGuardia Pl. (Bleecker/3rd) 646-654-6751

Young fashionistas in search of party attire can find nicely designed clothes here at moderate prices. Purdy Girl is the perfect place to play dress-up in styles that range from dressy jeans with rhinestone seams to a taffeta bubble-skirt that's an update of your mom's ballroom skirt.

· *Long pink taffeta bubble-skirt by Maxou $102*

· **Christa** · **Isabelle Fiore** · **Maxou** · **Ank** · **Autumn Cashmere**
· **Blue Dragon** · **Brooklyn Handknits** · **Illia** · **Jean-Michel Cazabat**
· **Josephine Loka** · **Nanette Lepore** · **Pin Up** · **Single**
· **Tibi Hyland** · **Ticci Tonetto** · **Tracy Reese** · **Trina Turk** · **XIE**

☺ Sun-Th 11-8, F-Sat 11-12
Store credit w/in 7 days w/ receipt.

B+		A-		B-	

Ibiza
46 University Pl. (9th/10th) 212-533-4614

After a tour of this store, you may feel as if you've just taken a worldwide shopping trip. Ibiza is warm, colorful, and packed with festive dresses and skirts in an assortment of luxury fabrics imported from all over the globe.

· *Pleated ankle-length skirt by Lilith $395*

· **Betsey Johnson** · **Ghost** · **Hanuman-Ganesh** · **Ibiza** · **Lilith**

☺ M-Sat 11-8, Sun 12:30-6:30
Store credit w/in 7 days.

B		B+		A-	

La Petite Coquette
51 University Pl. (9th/10th) 212-473-2478

The best lingerie store in Manhattan, La Petite Coquette is a mecca for lingerie lovers around the city. No wonder it's a favorite of celebrities like Sarah Jessica Parker, Cindy Crawford, and Naomi Campbell.

· *Sybaris sheer tulle shelf-bra $129 and thong $49*

· **Aubade** · **Christies** · **Cosabella** · **Delfina** · **Elle of Italy**
· **Fifi Chachnil** · **Gloria del Rio** · **Hanro** · **Huit** · **Janet Reger**
· **La Perla** · **Lise Charmelle** · **Marie Jo** · **Natori** · **Petit Bateau**
· **Prima Donna** · **Ravage** · **Rigby & Peller** · **Samantha Chang**
· **Silks** · **Simone Perele** · **Sybaris** · **Wacoal**

☺ M-Sat 11-7, Th 11-8, Sun 12-6
Store credit w/in 7 days.

B+		B		A	

BROADWAY

EMS
611 Broadway   (Houston/Bleecker)   212-505-9860

Camping fanatics will be thrilled to find an entire store dedicated to outdoor wear in the heart of Manhattan. EMS carries a solid selection of the most popular and durable outdoor attire, including ski parkas, fleece pants, and rugged backpacks. Anyone who feels like getting closer to nature can stop in here to gear up first.

· *North Face nylon shell $345*

· **EMS** · **Ex Officio** · **Gramicci** · **North Face**

🕐 M-F 10-9, Sat 10-8, Sun 12-6
Refund to method of payment
anytime w/ receipt or ID.

| B | B | B+ | |

Urban Outfitters
628 Broadway   (Houston/ Bleecker)   212-475-0009

In the past few years Urban Outfitters has practically become synonymous with young, current style, and this branch store doesn't disappoint. Catering to a surprisingly wide range of women, it brings integrity to trendiness.

· *Billy Blue recycled denim shirts $54*

· **Bulldog** · **Co-op** · **Diesel** · **Free People** · **Henna** · **Lux**
· **Melissa M** · **Mooks** · **Unitry B.** · **Urban Outfitters**

🕐 M-Sat 10-10, Sun 12-8
Refund w/in 7 days w/ receipt.

| C- | B- | B | |

Atrium
644 Broadway   (@ Bleecker)   212-473-9200

This spacious, modern store carries popular labels and classic basics by upscale streetwear designers. Fatten up your wardrobe with Atrium's traditional wool turtlenecks, trendy brand-name jeans, and cute tees. **Best Find: DKNY white cotton duck pants with sequins trim $245.**

· *Sergio Valente stone-washed denim jacket $190*

· **Diesel Style Lab** · **DKNY** · **Iceberg**
· **Levi's** · **Marithé François Girbaud** · **Parasuco**
· **Polo Sport** · **Sergio Valente**

🕐 M-Sat 10-9, Sun 11-8
Store credit w/in 14 days w/ receipt.

| C- | B | A- | |

Mikai
647 Broadway   (Bleecker/Bond)   212-529-8126

For working girls on a tight budget, Mikai supplies decent quality, cool styles, and reasonable prices for everything from suits to sexy little dresses. The sales at Mikai are amazing, so check in frequently to examine price tags.

· *Pink leather backless shirt $298*

· **Jerry Shabo** · **Mikai**

🕐 M-Sat 10:30-8:30, Sun 11:30-8:30
Store credit w/in 7 days w/ receipt.

| C+ | B- | B | |

service | presentation | quality | expense

Andy's Chee-Pees
691 Broadway   (3rd/4th)   212-420-5980

"Patience is a virtue." That should be your mantra while sifting through the cluttered, disorganized racks of second-hand clothing at Andy's Chee-Pees. College students and thrift shop fanatics will be thrilled with the used Levis, suede and leather jackets, and retro evening dresses. **Best Find: 1928 seafoam-green ankle-length velvet dress $600.**

· *Levi's 501's $45*

· **N/A**

☺ M-Sat 11-9, Sun 12-8
All sales final.

B- | C- | C+ |

Basic Basic
710 Broadway   (4th/Washington Pl.)   212-477-5711

Basic Basic is one of the best places to stock up on (you guessed it) the basics, especially quality cotton T-shirts. With enough styles and brands to suit the pickiest shopper, it's a place to shop, not browse. The trendier pieces are very predictable, so stick to the basic basics.

· *3 Dots long-sleeve tee $38*

· **3 Dots · Buffalo · Bulldog · Co-op · Fiorucci Jeans**
· **Free People · Free People · Jane Doe · Juicy Couture**
· **Mavi · Mes Dessous · Michael Stars · Petit Bateau**
· **Sweet Romeo · Y London · Z. Cavaricci**

☺ M-Sat 11-8, Sun 12-7
Store credit w/in 10 days w/ receipt.

C+ | B+ | C+ |

Antique Boutique
712-714 Broadway   (4th/Astor Pl.)   212-995-5577

The days of cheap second-hand clothing are long gone at this well-known boutique. Today the racks are filled with young, edgy, must-have merchandise for trendsetters, including off-beat styles, unusual necklines, and experimental fabrics. The boutique show-cases a number of European designers and houses an extensive selection, including its famous second-hand clothing.

· *Olive green suede pants with embroidered waist*
  by Josephine Loka $365

· **Alexandre Hechovitch · Alicia Lawhon · Christoph Brioch**
· **Christophe Lemaire · Delphine Wilson · Fake**
· **Gomme · Harwood · Hoarse · Hut Up · Jenny Udale**
· **Jessica Ogden · Joe Casely-Hayeford · Joelynian**
· **Josephine Loka · Jurgi Persoons · Kaj Ani · Lieve van Gorp**
· **Mandarina Duck · Maria Chen · Melissa Curry**
· **Michelle Mason · Mimsie Carlysle · Nghiem · NY Industrie**
· **O · People Used To Dream About the Future · Preen**
· **Reinaldo Lourenco · Rubin Chapelle · Severun Riach**
· **Shelly Fox · SVO · United Bamboo**

☺ M-Sat 11-9, Sun 12-8
Store credit w/ receipt.

C- | B+ | B |

service | presentation | quality | expense

BLEECKER STREET

Tibet Arts & Crafts
197 Bleecker St.   (6th/MacDougal)   212-260-5880

This store is all about scarves. You'll find a lavish selection of relatively inexpensive two-toned and reversible pashmina shawls and scarves that can be worn for dressy events or with a tank top and jeans. They are exceptionally warm and double as great head wraps for the winter. Be sure to check out the selection of beautifully patterned silks, which could be next year's pashmina. **Best Find: Raw cotton two-toned dress $35.**

· *70/30% pashmina/silk shawl $178*
· **N/A**
☺ M-Th 11-9, F-Sun 11-10
Store credit w/in 30 days w/ receipt.

B-	C+	B	

Spooly D's
51 Bleecker St.   (Lafayette/Bowery)   212-598-4415

This shop is slightly schizophrenic. Most of the merchandise is trendy and safe with labels that you stumble upon in every other neighborhood shop. You'll also find more original dresses and skirts from less popular labels. But if you're still coming up empty, check out the vintage items on the back wall. **Best Find: Hoyt & Bond cotton shirt dress $150.**

· *Earl cords $128*
· **Aetty Na** · **Earl Jeans** · **Hoyt & Bond** · **Katayone Adeli**
· **Le Havlin Piro** · **Liz Williams** · **Mimsie Carlysle**
· **Rubin Chapelle** · **Wink**
☺ T-Sat 12-7
Store credit w/in 7 days, valid 1 year.
Vintage sales final.

B+	B-	B+	

Bond 07 by Selima
7 Bond St.   (Broadway/Lafayette)   212-677-8487

This large boutique is packed with stylish bags, scarves and clothing, and you have to work a little harder to not miss anything. Fun and color are the running theme in this store, where dyed lamb jackets, sequined Chinese gowns, and asymmetric suede skirts are the norm. From an unusual evening gown or an alternative to everyday sweaters, Bond 07 will outfit a chic new you. **Best Find: Chinese sequined dress $900.**

· *Thick wool sleeveless turtleneck sweater $250*
· **Andrea Stuart** · **Anna Sui** · **Bess** · **Bette Mueller** · **Bond 07**
· **Carla Dawn Behrle** · **Cashmere Studio** · **Catherine**
· **Claudia Rapisard** · **Colette Dinnigan** · **Dr. Boudoir** · **Frou**
· **Gimmick** · **Harumi** · **Lea Anne Wallis** · **Leyla** · **Maja**
· **Mapuche** · **Megan Park** · **Melinda Zoller**
· **Norman Smitterman** · **Paige Roberts** · **Patty Shelabarger**
· **Petro Zillia** · **Phyllis Leibowitz** · **Sarah Violet**
· **Trash-à-Porter** · **Ursule Beaugeste** · **Velvet** · **Victor Marc**
☺ M-Sat 11-7, Th 11-8, Sun 12-7
Exchange w/ receipt w/in 14 days.

A-	A-	A-	

service | presentation | quality | expense

Daryl K
21 Bond St. *(Lafayette/Bowery)* *212-777-0713*

Loyal to urban wear, Daryl K has developed a distinct style in her short career. Her clothes are consistently edgy and in sync with what the hippest urbanites lust after. The more straight and narrow crowd can pick up a pair of her great-fitting hip-hugger jeans or classic updates of 3/4 length oxfords. Warning: these pants run very, very small so don't be upset if you're wearing a much larger size than usual.

· *Knee-high leather boots $225*

· **Daryl K**

☺ M-Sat 11-7, Sun 12-6
Store credit w/in 10 days w/ receipt.

B-	B	B+	

Katayone Adeli
35 Bond St. *(Lafayette/Bowery)* *212-260-3500*

The enormous, stylish space creates a chic, streamlined atmosphere to match the collection. As an alternative to the typical items carried in smaller boutiques, the main store carries sexy chiffon evening dresses, long wool dresses for work and dinners, chic suits, and trendier separates. **Best Find: Green chiffon dress $458.**

· *Cords $120*

· **Katayone Adeli**

☺ M-Sat 11-7, Sun 12-6
Store credit w/in 14 days w/ receipt.

C+	A	A-	

Leather Master
51 West 8th St. *(5th/6th)* *212-228-4997*

Everything at Leather Master has a price tag, but the prices appear to be negotiable. The merchandise is the usual selection of black and brown leather goods in a variety of cuts and sizes. Jackets are the best bet.

· *Mid-thigh-length jacket $249*

· **Ambition · Dimension · Leather Master**

☺ M-Sat 11-9, Sun 12-9
Exchange w/in 7 days w/ receipt.

B	B	A-	

Know Style
44 West 8th St. *(5th/6th)* *212-529-7655*

Know Style is probably a no-no once you're old enough to vote, but a definite yes-yes for hip younger teens looking for super savvy NYC club gear at low prices. The cheese factor is high, but if you take your time, you might find a knockout knockoff. **Best Find: Nally & Millie red backless halter with zebra trim $40.**

· *Cotton tank with sequins straps $20*

· **Dop · Jane Doe · Ju Cunda · Just in Time · Lani**
· **Lucent · Matrix · Nissi · Paloma Picasso · Parasuco**
· **Sans Souci · Scott Clothing · Sin · Sole Mio · Sooki**
· **Tripp · Via 101 · XOXO**

☺ M-T 11-9, F-Sat 11-10, Sun 12-9
Exchange w/in 7 days w/ receipt.

C+	C+	C+	

service | presentation | quality | expense

Petit Peton
27 West 8th St.   (5th/6th)   212-677-3730

In this store, shoes are the main event. Even basic black shoes and boots in this shop demand notice—though not quite as insistently, of course, as the stiletto heels. Made with materials such as feathers, fur, and beads, the shoes are sometimes totally over the top but lovable nonetheless.

· *Claudio Marazzi wedge-heeled mule with white mink strap and sequinned sole $398*

· **Casadei** · **Debut** · **Fantini** · **Gianmarco Lorenzi**
· **Giuseppe Zanotti** · **NCI** · **Nello Nembo** · **Ordinary People**
· **Patrick Cox** · **Pedro Garcia** · **RAS** · **René Caovilla** · **Sky**
· **SXY** · **Vicini** · **Vis à Vis**

☺ M-Sat 11-9, Sun 12-8
Store credit w/in 7 days w/ receipt.

   B | **B** | **B+** |

Untitled
26 West 8th St.   (5th/6th)   212-505-9725

Untitled is a beacon of couture style among the bevy of cheap and trendy stores that line Eighth Street. It carries only the best young and current designers and never shies away from the unknown label or the provocative design. All this excitement comes with a hefty price tag, so the ideal customer here is both adventurous and financially secure.

· *Allesandro dell'Acqua mesh embroidered shirt with sweater cuffs and collar $578*

· **3 Dots** · **6 by Martin Margiela** · **AA Milano**
· **Alessandro Dell'Acqua** · **Alexander McQueen**
· **Catherine** · **Custo** · **D&G** · **Fendi** · **Helmut Lang**
· **Iceberg** · **Jean Paul Gaultier** · **Martin Margiela**
· **Moschino** · **Plein Sud** · **Sergio Valente**
· **Veronique Branquinho** · **Vivienne Westwood**
· **Yigal Azrouel**

☺ M-Sat 11:30-9, Sun 12-9
Store Credit w/in 7 days w/ receipt.
Sale items final.

  B+ | **B+** | **A** |

JD
1 West 8th St.   (5th/6th)   212-533-7222

Look beyond the tube tops. You'll find evening wear that's not only sexy, but also mature and tasteful. Synthetic fabrics and faux-fur items are everywhere but leather pants and knit sweaters are the real stand-outs.

· *Faux-fur cropped vest $109*

· **JD** · **Jeffrey Scott** · **Parallel**

☺ M-Sat 11-8:30, Sun 12-7:30
Exchange w/in 7 days w/ receipt.

  B | **B-** | **A-** |

service | presentation | quality | expense

Patricia Fields
10 East 8th St.   *(5th/University)*   *212-254-1699*

The last bastion of true Greenwich Village spirit, Patricia Fields offers one of the most memorable shopping experiences in New York. The sales help is as colorful as the clothing and the boutique looks like a drag queen's closet, filled with fun sexy clothing for the truly fabulous. High school girls love the daring selection, as do downtown partiers looking for a sequined micro-mini or a feather boa. **Best Find: Rough-edged, paint-splattered leather halter-top with open back $168.**

· *Open-knit mohair sweater, mid-calf with hood, by Foley $155*

· **Ann Hitchcock · Carla Dawn Behrle · Catherine**
· **Cesar Arellanes · Cheryl Creations · Cheyenne · Clutch**
· **Corey Lynn Calter · David Dalrymple · Deviations · E.C. Star**
· **Flux · Foley · Hushi Robot · Illia · Kazumi · Lip Service**
· **Margie Tsai · MEA Fashion · Michael Sears · Mighty Atom**
· **Miss Sixty · Petra Barraza · Rebecca Dannenberg · Rona**
· **Ruisi · Serious · Silvia Petra · Sue Wong · Syren**

☉ Sun-W 12-8, Th-Sat 12-9
Store credit w/in 10 days w/ receipt.
Sales final on lingerie and accessories.

   B+ | **B+** | **B-** |

East Village

A. Cheng
Anna
Back From Guatemala
Blue
Daryl K*
Dö Kham Emporium
Dress Shoppe
Eileen Fisher*
Gap*
Gin Gin
Horn
Jill Anderson
Jutta Neuman
Kimono House
Leather Rose
Lord of the Fleas*
Mark Montano
Meghan Kinney
Min-K
Mode
No XS
Red Tape by Rebecca Dannenberg
Resurrection*
Selia Yang
Studio 109
Sway
Tibet Arts and Crafts
Tokio 7
Tokyo Joe
Urban Outfitters*

*Additional locations can be found
in the Multiple Store Index pp.152-159.

EAST THIRD STREET

Anna
150 East 3rd St.   (Ave.A/Ave.B)   **212-358-0195**

This is the kind of store which can lead even the most practical into the Valley of the Impulse Buy. Nothing here is vital or even practical, for that matter. There are some special items, though, like alligator-print velvet pants or off-kilter sweaters that suit any young, hip woman.

· *Kathy Kemp velour crocodile-print pants $120*
· **Kathy Kemp**
☺ M-F 1-8, Sat-Sun 1-7
Store credit w/in 3 days.

     B | B- | C+ |

Gin Gin
193 East 4th St.   (Ave.A/Ave.B)   **212-979-1966**

A few pieces of colorful clothes fill this tiny shop. Though the prices seem reasonable at first glance, the amateurish finish makes the merchandise too expensive for the quality. Shirts in particular lack finesse, but in the case of the wraparound skirts, colorful patterns make up for the lack of detailing.

· *Jersey sleeveless top $50*
· **Gin Gin**
☺ T-Sat 1-8, Sun 1-7
All sales final.

     C+ | C+ | B |

Dress Shoppe
218 East 5th St.   (2nd/3rd)   **212-260-4963**

The unassuming name of this boutique doesn't begin to describe what awaits you. Fully stocked with exquisite new and antique skirts, saris, shawls and bedspreads imported from India, Dress Shoppe could be Manhattan's best-kept secret. Closely examine the shawls to truly appreciate their exquisite fabrics and attention to detail, and just for thrills, request to see the 150-year-old beaded skirts and bedspreads.

· *Antique Indian shawls $50-$130*
· **N/A**
☺ M-Sat 11-9
Exchange only.

     A | B | B+ |

Dö Kham Emporium
304 East 5th St.   (1st/2nd)   **212-358-1010**

The best Tibetan shop in Manhattan is a scarf/shawl haven filled with exquisite Pashminas in a gorgeous array of primary and pastel colors as well as mohair boas, silk-dyed shawls, and stunning floor length wrap-skirts. It also carries matching raw silk bags, Tibetan-style cotton shirts, and exquisite bed covers, pillowcases and wall hangings.

· *Tibetan cotton $35*
· **N/A**
☺ M-Sun 11-8
Store credit w/in 14 days.

     B- | B+ | A- |

Daryl K
208 East 6th St. (2nd/3rd) 212-475-1255

If downtown girls had a uniform, Daryl K would be the place to find it. This hole-in-the-wall outlet offers a smattering of mismatched and poorly organized sale items from the designer's previous seasons' collections. The lower prices make rummaging through the garbage can bins worthwhile.

· *Cotton khakis $59*

· **Daryl K**

☉ M-Sat 12-7, Sun 12-6
Store credit for items carried at main store.
Sales final on all other items.

B- | C+ | B+ |

Back From Guatemala
306 East 6th St. (1st/2nd) 212-260-7010

Back From Guatemala is for a Birkenstock kind of woman. It carries a good selection of rough-woven textile clothing, imported from all over the world. If the clothes aren't your style, check out the jewelry.

· *Linen embroidered shirt $58*

· **Arise · Cut Loose · Flax · Red Dragonfly**

☉ M-Sun 12-11:30
Store credit w/in 14 days w/ tags and receipt.

B | C+ | C+ |

Tokio 7
64 East 7th St. (1st/2nd) 212-353-8443

Dark, dingy and a little musty, Tokio 7 is the chicest consignment shop downtown, and for the most part the clothes are as affordable as you'd hope they'd be. Gaultier, Prada, and Daryl K are just a few of the seriously high-fashion hand-me-downs you might encounter.

· *Paul Smith pants $65*

· **N/A**

☉ M-Sun 12-8:30
All sales final.

C- | C+ | B+ |

No-XS
80 East 7th St. (1st/2nd) 212-674-6753

"Will give knitting lessons" reads the sign that hangs in the front of this custom-knit sweater shop. If you don't have the time or patience to knit yourself a sweater, the owner of this shop will do the job at a moderate expense. A perfect solution to the grievous problem of favorite sweater death.

· *Knit strapless tube top $45*

· **No-XS · Philleo**

☉ M 1-6, Tu-F 12-8, Sat 12-9
Store credit w/in 7 days.

C+ | C | B- |

EAST SEVENTH STREET

Sway

84 East 7th St. (1st/2nd) 212-505-0490

At Sway you'll pay a pretty penny for that arts-and-crafts-project-gone-awry look: pants with seams revealed, shirts with necklines cut off, and tattered-looking dresses. The risk of the deconstructed look, of course, is that people won't realize it's on purpose; but if that's not a problem, get into the swing at Sway.

· *Grey wool pants $320*

· **Sway**

☺ M-Sun 12-8
Store credit w/in 7 days.

| C | | C- | | C+ | | |

Kimono House

93 East 7th St. (1st/Ave.A) 212-505-0232

Whether you wear them or hang them on your wall, kimonos make an elegant and dramatic statement. At this shoe-box size store, both new and antique kimonos are sold for reasonable prices.

· *Vintage silk kimono $369*

· **N/A**

☺ M-Sat 1-7, Sun 1-6
Exchange w/in 14 days w/ receipt.

| B | | C | | A- | | |

Resurrection

123 East 7th St. (1st/Ave.A) 212-228-0063

Resurrection is the shop where grandma's clothes come back to life. The hand-me-downs are arranged in an orderly fashion, and the racks are often filled with pieces that you might find in the editorial layouts of this month's fashion magazines. This season, for example, there is an ample supply of crocheted shawls and jean skirts. Because of the excellent condition and the unusually high style, the clothes here are a bit pricier than at other vintage stores.

· *Pucci cotton shirt $225*

· **N/A**

☺ M-Sat 1-9, Sun 1-8
All sales final.

| C | | B+ | | B- | | |

Mode

109 St. Mark's Pl. (1st/Ave.A) 212-529-9208

Mode keeps its customer up to date by packing the space with young, fun and trendy clothing. Here fleece is used in a new context: as material for wrap dresses/coats. There are also pretty chiffon blouses to lighten up any evening outfit. Those looking for trends but unwilling to dress exactly like everyone else may find Mode to be the perfect shopping spot.

· *Matching fleece jacket $78, and pants $38*

· **Albert Chan · Beautiful People · Buqet · Bond · Cesar Arellanes · Luxe · Mimi Turner · Plum · Scott Gibson · Tae Hyun · Tessa Oh**

☺ M-Sun 12-9
Store credit w/in 5 days.

| C+ | | B- | | B+ | | |

Studio 109
115 St. Marks Pl.   *(1st/Ave.A)*   **212-420-0077**

This store has turned out sexy, custom-made leather fashions for such celebrity clients as Jennifer Lopez and Lauren Hill. Though it claims to dress mainly superstars, if you make an appointment they'll dress little old you, too. The leather is available in many different colors and is super soft.

· *Leather halter top $125*

· **Hybrid** · **Studio 109**

☺ M-Sun 12-8
Store credit w/in 15 days w/ receipt.
Alterations free on custom.

    B | **C+** | **A** |

Blue
125 St. Mark's Pl.   *(1st/Ave.A)*   **212-228-7744**

There's only one major flaw with this great find of a store: the customer may develop asthma over the course of her fittings due to the constant haze of cigarette smoke. Custom dresses are Blue's specialty. A large selection of floor samples can be made in any color or material. Or if you have your own vision in mind, custom-design your own dress and Blue will make that dream gown a reality.

· *Raw silk bridesmaid's dress $400*

· **Blue**

☺ M-Sat 12-7:30, Sun 12-5:30
Store credit w/in 3 months w/ receipt.

    B+ | **C-** | **A-** |

Lord of the Fleas
305 East 9th St.   *(1st/2nd)*   **212-260-9130**

For a cheap thrill, dress yourself up for a night or two on the town with an outfit from Lord of the Fleas. The funky styles and cheap stretch fabrics won't outlast any trend, but the young and fickle who want to reinvent themselves overnight shouldn't mind.

· *T-shirts with kitschy prints $22*

· **Bulldog** · **Cheryl Creations** · **Flyby** · **Free People**
· **Friends Design Group** · **Hourglass** · **Illig** · **Kangol**
· **Lord of the Fleas** · **Lord of the Fleas** · **Retango** · **Survival**
· **Z. Cavaricci** · **Zoom**

☺ M-Sat 12-8
Store credit w/in 7 days w/ receipt.

    C- | **C-** | **C+** |

Meghan Kinney
312 East 9th St.   *(1st/2nd)*   **212-260-6329**

This is one store in the East Village that promises wearable attire without compromising individuality. Kinney uses traditional fabrics but adds unexpected touches, so that a little turtleneck can turn into a funnel-neck and a knee-length skirt has a ruffle around the hem.

· *Wool skirt $125*

· **Meghan Kinney**

☺ M-Sat 12-8, Sun 12-6
Exchange w/ receipt.

    C+ | **C+** | **B** |

EAST NINTH STREET

Jutta Neuman
317 East 9th St. (1st/2nd) 212-982-7048

Jutta Neuman is a cobbler in the most authentic sense. She designs and will custom-make shoes, bags, belts and wallets. Neuman uses the finest leathers in matte or shiny finishes and colors ranging from vibrant to subtle and natural. **Best Find: Pony cardholder $35.**

· *Turquoise leather tote bag $185*

· **Jutta Neuman**

⊙ T-Sat 12-8
Store credit w/in 10 days. Custom orders final.

   C- | C+ | A- |

Selia Yang
328 East 9th St. (1st/2nd) 212-254-9073

Playing dress-up couldn't be more bizarre than it is at Selia Yang. A parrot sits perched atop an enormous cage and watches you peruse the racks of refreshing classic-with-spunk evening wear. Look for column dresses studded with sparkling rhinestones, at prices that reflect the quality. **Best Find: Beaded green silk column dress $700.**

· *Silk organza knee-length skirt $150*

· **Selia Yang**

⊙ T-F 1-8, Sat-Sun 12-6
Store credit w/in 7 days.

   C+ | B | A- |

Horn
328 East 9th St. (1st/2nd) 212-358-0213

With its sunken floor covered entirely in pebbles, this store makes something truly special out of a small space. The über-chic downtown gang will love its small selection of items from successful, innovative designers. Sweaters with cut-out sleeves and asymmetric dresses are typical fare.

· *Pierrot red wool sleeveless turtleneck $275*

· **Alexander McQueen · Asfour · Claudia Hill · Dugg · Givenchy · Markus Huemer · Pierrot**

⊙ T-Sat 1-8, Sun 2-8
Exchange w/ receipt w/in 7 days.

   C+ | A- | A- |

Jill Anderson
331 East 9th St. (1st/2nd) 212-253-1747

A great find for all women who appreciate simple clothing made with up-to-date fabrics. Look for the occasional formal dress and tops and bottoms in stretchy wool that resembles fleece. The store does alterations, so whatever doesn't appear to have been made for your body can be coaxed into line. **Best Find: Satin ankle-length bias cut dress $185.**

· *Wool tube top $145*

· **Jill Anderson**

⊙ M-Sun 12-9
Store credit valid 1 year.

   B+ | B+ | B |

service | presentation | quality | expense

Red Tape by Rebecca Dannenberg
333 East 9th St.   (1st/2nd)   212-529-8483

Downtown girls call these clothes standard fare. Upper East Side girls think they're edgy. Such is the boundary-crossing potential of Rebecca Dannenberg's designs, which are for the skinny and financially secure (though the Red Tape label is her cheaper line). Her trademark bootleg pants, thin knit cardigans and other urban-chic garments are, for the most part, timeless and seasonless, so you might feel that they're worth the price.

· *Cotton pants $110*

· **Rebecca Dannenberg · Red Tape**

☺ M-T 12-7, W-Sun 12-8
Store credit w/in 10 days.

| C+ | | B | | A- | | |

Leather Rose
412 East 9th St.   (1st/Ave.A)   212-529-6790

Although the initial vibe of this store may remind you of the leather shop in *Seven* (that will make anything you desire in leather), the clothes here are pretty harmless. Custom pants come in a variety of leathers and can be made from any pair of pants you bring in to be copied, whatever the style.

· *Leather pants $700*

· **N/A**

☺ T-Sun 1-8
All sales final.

| B+ | | B- | | B+ | | |

Mark Montano
434 East 9th St.   (1st/Ave.A)   212-505-0325

The eponymous owner of this closet-sized boutique just might be the next big cutting-edge couture designer. Mark Montano laughs in the face of minimalism by mixing old-school classics with modern-day edge and humor. The result: hot pink crepe suits with black lace from the knee down, custom corsets in wild colors, and more. **Best Find: Jersey sleeveless turtleneck $80.**

· *Hot pink/black crepe lace suit, jacket and pants $125 each*

· **Mark Montano**

☺ T-Fri 11-7
Store credit w/in 7 days.

| B+ | | C+ | | B | | |

A. Cheng
443 East 9th St.   (1st/Ave.A)   212-979-7324

East Village shopkeepers who whip up creations in the back of the store often turn out clothes that resemble something an angst-ridden teenager might make in home-ec. Not so at this tiny shop. The ultra-soft handmade clothes are of the finest quality and can add verve to any outfit.

· *Super-fine button-down shirt $88*

· **A. Cheng**

☺ M-F 1-8, Sat-Sun 12-8
Store credit w/in 7 days.

| B | | B+ | | B | | |

EAST ELEVENTH STREET

Tokyo Joe
334 East 11th St.   (1st/2nd)   212-473-0724

The cramped space makes it difficult to appreciate the jam-packed racks of upscale resale clothing. Tokyo Joe carries clothing and accessories along the lines of Prada and Joseph. High school girls and college fashion plates on a modest budget can find beautiful designs at affordable prices. Beggars can be choosers at Tokyo Joe, but only if they've got the style to turn last year's clothes into this year's fashion statement.

· *Gucci Jeans $95*

· **N/A**

☺ M-Sun 12-9
All sales final.

    C | C- | B+ |

Min-K
334 East 11th St.   (1st/2nd)   212-253-8837

Everything in this sleek store is either imported from Korea or Japan or designed by the owner. The clothes are hung on slanted racks, and giant fluorescent lights illuminate the space, so the young and fashion-conscious can easily spot the next cool thing. You won't see any of these clothes anywhere else, so your wardrobe can be as one-of-a-kind as you are.

· *Asymmetric skirt $130*

· **Knick Knack · Min-K by Minji Kim · Sugar · Tomoko Igarashi**

☺ M-Sun 12:30-8:30
Store credit w/in 7 days w/ receipt.

    A- | A- | B |

Soho

Agnès B.	Furla	Patagonia
A.P.C.	Harriet Love	Pearl River*
A/X Armani Exchange*	Helmut Lang	Peter Hermann
Add	Heun	Phat Farm
Alice Underground	Hotel Venus	Philosophy di
Alpana Bawa	IF	Alberta Ferretti
Anna Sui	INA*	Pierre Garroudi
Anne Fontaine	Institut*	Pleats Please
Anthropologie*	J.Crew*	Plein Sud
Arizona	Jill Stuart	Polo Sport*
Bagutta	Joseph (pant store)*	Prada Sport
Banana Republic*	Juno*	Product
Barbara Bui	Kate Spade	Putumayo
Bebesh	Keiko	Rampage
Betsy Johnson*	Kenneth Cole*	René Lezard
Big Drop*	Kirna Zabête	Riva Mirasager
Bisou Bisou	Laundry by Shelli	Rose Ann's
Calypso on Broome	Segal	Sacco*
Canal Jeans	Le Corset	Scoop*
Catherine	Legacy	Sharagano
Chuckies*	Louie	Shin Choi/Coleridge
Club Monaco*	Louis Vuitton*	Sisley
Coach*	M-A-G	Steven Alan
Costume National	Malo	Su-Zen
Country Road*	Manrico	Tehen
Cynthia Rowley	Marc Jacobs	The Orginal Leather
D&G	Marianne	Store*
Daang Goodman	Novobotsky	Tocca
Daffy's*	Mavi	Todd Oldham
David Aaron	Max Studio	Varda*
Dawn Ebony Martin	Mikai*	Ventilo
Debra Moorefield	Miu Miu	Via Spiga
Deco Jewels	Morgane Le Fay*	Victoria's Secret*
Detour*	Morgane Le Fay Home	Vivienne Tam
Diesel Style Lab	Mystique Boutique	Vivienne Westwood
Dosa	Nakazawa	What Comes Around
E. Vogel Boots	New York Look*	Goes Around
& Shoes	Nicole Miller*	XOXO
Eileen Fisher*	Nine West*	Yaso
Epperson Studio	Oasis	Yellow Rat Bastard
F by Fortuna Valentino	Old Navy*	YL by Yair
Freelance	Otto Tootsi Plohound	Yohji Yamamoto
French Connection*	Paracelso	Yvonne Christa
French Corner		Zabari

*Additional locations can be found
in the Multiple Store Index pp. 152-159.

service | presentation | quality | expense

SULLIVAN STREET

Tibet Arts & Crafts
144 Sullivan St.   *(Houston/Prince)*   212-529-4344

You'll find a lavish selection of relatively inexpensive two-toned and reversible pashmina shawls and scarves that can be worn for dressy events or with a tank top and jeans. Be sure to check out the selection of beautifully patterned silks, which could be next year's pashmina. **Best Find: Woven silk brocade purse with Buddha print $9.**

· *Two-toned pashmina shawl with beaded collar $265*

· **N/A**

☺ M-Sun 11-8
Store credit w/in 30 days w/ receipt.

B- | C+ | B | 🐷 2

Pierre Garroudi
139 Thompson St.   *(Houston/Prince)*   212-475-2333

Custom dresses in 24 hours. Enough said! The designer will cater to your every whim by whipping up a dream dress based on a sketch, a picture from a magazine or a hopelessly shabby favorite. You can also choose from the beautiful samples within the shop. If the fabrics on hand are not to your liking, you may supply your own or ask for directions to the owner's fabric source. All tastes and sizes can be accommodated.

· *Orange strapless viscose/taffeta gown $1400*

· **Pierre Garroudi**

☺ M-Sun 10-8
All sales final.

A | B | A- | 🐷 3

Nakazawa
137 Thompson St.   *(Houston/Prince)*   212-505-7768

Hard-to-find plus-size kimonos and other Asian imports are available in this tiny, unadorned emporium. Nakazawa caters to all sizes with Japanese-style jackets and colorful sweaters as well as kimonos.

· *Silk kimono $330*

· **Nakazawa**

☺ M-Sat 11-8, Sun 11-7:30
All sales final.

B- | C- | B | 🐷 2

Deco Jewels
131 Thompson St.   *(Houston/Prince)*   212-253-1222

Deco Jewels showcases a collection of lucite bags made between 1949 and 1959. Available in many colors, shapes and sizes, the bags can become part of an eclectic evening ensemble. Also here: cufflinks and rhinestone jewelry dating from the Victorian era to the 1960s.

· *Vintage lucite bag $250*

· **N/A**

☺ M-Sun 12-8
Store credit w/in 14 days.

A+ | A- | A+ | 🐷 3

Peter Hermann
118 Thompson St.   (Prince/Spring)   212-966-9050

Tiny and over-loaded with bags, Peter Hermann's maximum occupancy cannot exceed four customers. The merchandise is standard but good for the conservative professional woman who wants a little style along with functionality.

· *Large dyed pony-hair bag $490*

· **Desmo** · **Jamin Puech** · **Les Copains** · **Mandarina Duck**
· **Paule Ka** · **Raffe** · **Strenesse** · **Tardini**

☺ M-Sat 12-7, Sun 1-6
Store credit.

A | **C-** | **A-** |

Sacco
111 Thompson St.   (Prince/Spring)   212-925-8010

Although the selection here consists mainly of the store's own label, Sacco also carries a small but great selection of popular shoe lines. You can always find the most up-to-date styles here. At the moment that means Audrey Hepburn-type flats or patent loafers with a chunky heel. **Best Find: Marc Jacobs knock-off flats $149**.

· *Classic loafers $149*

· **Aquatalia** · **Bettye Mueller** · **Claudia Ciuti** · **Cynthia Rowley**
· **Gretel's Clogs** · **Hobo** · **Jean-Michel Cazabat** · **Laura** · **Maxx**
· **Nancy Nancy** · **NM7O** · **RAS** · **Sacco** · **Wosh**

☺ M-F 11-8, Sat 11-7, Sun 12-7

Refund w/in 10 days w/ receipt.

B | **A-** | **A-** |

Dawn Ebony Martin
110 Thompson St.   (Prince/Spring)   212-334-6479

Take two for the price of one literally at this store. Nearly everything is reversible, and prices are great. The wrap-around styles in raw silks and linens make chic ethnic evening apparel that anyone would love. But try them on: they look less complicated on a body than on a hanger. **Best Find: Super-thick cashmere shawl with fringe bottom $195**.

· *Reversible silk wrap evening top $135*

· **Dawn Ebony Martin**

☺ M-Sat 12-7, Sun 1-6
Exchange w/in 4 days.

B | **B+** | **A-** |

Legacy
109 Thompson St.   (Prince/Spring)   212-966-4827

Though the limited selection of vintage items and accessories give Legacy its feel, its true personality is downtown and edgy. The owners focus on fit and quality with style, guaranteeing you'll not leave their eclectic store empty-handed.

· *James Coviello sweater $232*

· **Agneta Eckemyr** · **Claudio Orchiani** · **Coup de Pied**
· **Gabrielle Hamil** · **James Coviello** · **Lee Jane**
· **Sabine Schmidt** · **Stella Cadente** · **Whistles**

☺ M-Sun 12-7
Store credit w/in 7 days w/ receipt.

A- | **B-** | **A-** |

THOMPSON STREET

Dosa
107 Thompson St.   (Prince/Spring)   212-431-1733

If you blink, you might miss this tiny store. Dosa specializes in subtly beautiful clothing such as velvet Chinese-pajama-inspired tops, skirts and pants. Bolder shoppers will love the delicate gauze blouses and wool tie-dyed shawls in rainbow colors. **Best Find: Wool shawls $140.**

· *Chinese velvet pajamas, top $260, pants $235*
· **Dosa**

☺ M-Sat 12-7, Sun 12-6
Store credit w/in 10 days w/ receipt.

B- | **B** | **A-**

INA
101 Thompson St.   (Prince/Spring)   212-941-4757

Hand-me downs have never been so chic. This designer resale shop houses an amazing selection of barely-worn clothing from the rich and stylish. For those who can't pay high-fashion prices the first time around, here's a second chance.

· *Leather Prada bag $350*
· **N/A**

☺ M-Sun 12-7
All sales final.

C+ | **B-** | **A-**

Le Corset
80 Thompson St.   (Spring/Broome)   212-334-4936

For a touch of Paris, stop by this cozy lingerie store. You'll find playful undergarments that say, "Voulez-vouz coucher avec moi?" (or words to that effect). Le Corset also features great tops to wear for nights on the town, blending traditional corset styles with new materials like stretch velvet and chiffon.

· *Chiffon/velvet corset $195*

· **Andre Sarda** · **Aubade** · **Chantal Thomas** · **Colette Dinnigan**
· **Corine Gilson** · **Dr. Boudoir** · **Ellen Berkenblit** · **Le Corset**
· **Leigh Bantivoglio** · **Lise Charmelle** · **Nina Ricci** · **Selima Lingerie**

☺ M-Sat 11-7, Th 11-8, Sun 12-7
Store credit w/in 10 days w/ receipt.

B | **B+** | **B+**

Louie
68 Thompson St.   (Spring/Broome)   212-274-1599

This colorful boutique, with its semi-circular rack of eclectic clothes, is a perfect shop for any twenty-something looking for a cute frock. Whether it's a long red wool-and-cashmere coat or a shift-style dress, a piece of clothing from Louie will never make you look like a conformist. **Best Find: Aqcua wool/cashmere coat $600.**

· *Bloom bag $140*

· **Acqua** · **Bloom** · **Cassanova** · **Gabriella Zanzani**
· **Julien Segura** · **Lauren Moffatt** · **New Scotland** · **Rosa Nichols**
· **Sabine Schmidt** · **Stephen Di Geronimo** · **Yoon**

☺ T-Sat 12-7, Sun 12-6
Store credit w/in 5 days.

C+ | **B** | **A-**

Epperson Studio
25 Thompson St. (Watts/Grand) 212-226-3181

Epperson Studio feels more like a tailor's shop than a ready-to-wear boutique. Rich fabrics are combined with unfinished hemlines to create off-kilter evening wear. Most designs—like the deep-red velvet strapless gown with rough denim trim—will appeal only to downtown girls.

· *Gowns $710*

· **Epperson**

🕐 T-Sat 1-8
Exchange w/in 30 days w/ receipt.
Special orders sales final.

| A- | C | B | |

Bisou Bisou
474 West Broadway (Houston/Prince) 212-260-9640

The Soho location gives this line of otherwise tragically trendy clothing a bit of class. The trick with this store is to buy only pieces and avoid making an "outfit."

· *Long black-lined dress $118*

· **Bisou Bisou**

🕐 M-Sat 11-8, Sun 12-7
Refund w/in 14 days w/ tags and receipt.

| B | B | B- | |

Detour
472 West Broadway (Houston/ Prince) 212-979-6315

Dance music is always blaring at this boutique and the "security guard" looks like a bouncer. Though the selection ranges from stylish and expensive labels to flat-out Euro-cheese, a discerning browser might find some keepers—such as camel-hair pants with satin trim. But these clothes don't come cheap.

· *Stephen Di Geronimo satin-trimmed camel-hair pants $235*

· **Wu's · Absolu · Aquah · Big Star · Blakes · Buzz 18 · Cheyenne · Cop Copains · Curiositees · Dimension · f.a.l. · Hamnett · Juicy Couture · Link · M Collection · Michel Klein · Pinko · Poleci · Rozae Nichols · Severine Peraudin · State of the Heart · Stephen Di Geronimo · Sweet Pea**

🕐 M-Sun 11-8
Store credit w/in 7 days w/ receipt.

| C | B+ | A- | |

Sisley
469 West Broadway (Houston/Prince) 212-375-0538

Sisley offers a dependable line of basics to accommodate both the office and cocktail hour. Reasonably priced to begin with, this great clothing is an out-and-out steal when it goes on sale. Stop in from time to time to check the bargains and the new arrivals.

· *Mid-calf wool skirt $98*

· **Sisley**

🕐 M-Sat 11-8, Sun 11-6
Refund w/in 14 days w/ tag and receipt.
Store credit afterwards.

| C+ | B | B+ | |

service | presentation | quality | expense

The New York Look
468 West Broadway (Houston/Prince) 212-598-9988

Perhaps this store would have been better named "The New York Attitude," which its nasty and pushy sales staff has in abundance. The store carries a fantastic selection of sophisticated popular fashions for Gen X-ers and Baby Boomers. But don't let the sales people pressure you into making a purchase you don't really want. **Best Find: Patrick Gerard mohair poncho $188.**

· *Wool pants $188*

· **Laundry · Patrick Gerard · Regina Rubens · Sara Koee**
· **Tahari · Teen Flo · Theory · Urchin · Whistles · William B**

☺ M-Sat 11-8, Th 11-9, Sun 12-8
Exchange w/in 7 days w/ receipt.

| D+ | B | A- | |

French Corner
464 West Broadway (Houston/Prince) 212-505-1980

Europe's most happening designs inhabit this crammed Soho space, where the racks of modish fashions run the gamut from work clothes to club gear. **Best Find: Daryl K micropleat cords $150.**

· *Nylon pants $200*

· **Anna Sui · Bazaar by Christian Lacroix · Chaiken & Capone**
· **Chip & Chic · D&G · Daryl K · Easel · Friponne · Future Ozbek**
· **Gianfranco Ferre · Iceberg · Indivi · Katayone Adeli · Lea Rome**
· **Lorena Conti · Maje · Moschino · NY Industrie · Paul & Joe**
· **Philosophy · Roberto Cavalli · Urchin · Versace · Versus**

☺ M-Sun 11-8
Exchange w/in 7 days w/ receipt.

| B | B- | A- | |

Add
461 West Broadway (Houston/Prince) 212-539-1439

Add is a small boutique packed with adorable purses for both day and night, along with fabulous costume jewelry and a wall of shawls—from plain to heavily beaded—to enhance any humdrum ensemble.

· *Adriene Landon beaded shawl $199*

· **Adriene Landon · Ben Amun · Cerruti 1881**
· **Francesco Biasia · Ilana Wolf · Kokin · Samoto**

☺ M-Sun 11-8
Exchange w/in 7 days. Sale items final.

| A- | B | B | |

YL by Yair
460 West Broadway (Houston/Prince) 212-254-5179

YL is the retail Valium for people who leave dress shopping to the last minute. Chock full of cocktail and formal dresses, the store will outfit you for any dressy occasion. But think costume, not heirloom: your purchase will get you through the night in question, but it probably won't last long after that. **Best Find: Black satin ballroom dress $198.**

· *Calf-length dress $168*

· **YL by Yair**

☺ M-Sat 11-7, Sun 12-7
Store credit w/in 7 days on casual wear only.

| C+ | B+ | C+ | |

SOHO

Philosophy di Alberta Ferretti
452 West Broadway (Houston/Prince) 212-460-5500

This store carries an oh-so-pretty line of delicate Italian knits and dresses that are very feminine in a modern way. The delicate shifts and delightful wool coats are especially desirable. **Best Find: Felt bag $110.**

· *Short wool/felt dress $495*

· **Philosophy di Alberta Ferretti**

☺ M-Sat 11-7, Sun 12-6
7 days exchange or store credit w/ receipt.

B+ | B+ | A |

French Connection
435 West Broadway (@ Prince) 212-219-1197

Long gone are the days of flimsy materials and fleeting styles at French Connection. The company now makes clothes which are clean-lined and modern; cool without screaming "trendoid"—in short, ideal work clothes. The winter line tends to be particularly strong. Wool-cashmere blends and other appealing fabrics are fashioned into wide-leg trousers, A-line knee-length skirts, and simple fitted sweaters, some great for play as well as work.

· *Waist-length nylon hooded jacket with
  detachable sleeves $178*

· **French Connection**

☺ M-Sat 11-9, Sun 11-8
Full refund w/in 7 days w/ receipt.
14 days if item on sale.

B- | A- | A- |

D&G
434 West Broadway (Prince/Spring) 212-965-8000

The secondary line from high-end designers Dolce & Gabbana is not as glamorous as the primary one, but it is a lot crazier--and a little too ostentatious. Slim women looking to spice up their wardrobes with an outfit that combines animal prints and multicolored stripes will appreciate the enormous selection at D&G. **Best Find: Neon press crocodile leather belts $55.**

· *Twill pants $230*

· **D&G**

☺ M-Sat 11-7, Sun 12-6
Store credit w/in 7 days w/ receipt.

B | A- | A |

Furla
430 West Broadway (Prince/Spring) 212-343-0048

A moderately-priced bag store that gives good style and good leather for the money, Furla is a perfect destination for career women who want a functional work bag that doubles as a chic fashion accessory.

· *Shopping-bag style with shoulder straps $145*

· **Furla**

☺ M-Sat 11-7, Sun 12-6
Store credit w/in 7 days.

B | A | A | (3)

WEST BROADWAY

XOXO
426 West Broadway   (Prince/Spring)   212-334-9450

A favorite of teens, XOXO carries a line of knock-off trendy clothes at reasonable prices. With all the matching pieces, you may be tempted to buy an ensemble. Resist, or you'll have XOXO written all over you. **Best Find: Satin ankle-length skirt $68.**

· *Velour pants $54*

· **XOXO**

☺ M-Th 11-8, F-Sat 11-9, Sun 11-7
Store credit w/in 7 days w/ receipt.

| B | B | C+ | 2 |

Bebesh
425 West Broadway   (Prince/Spring)   212-226-4969

The window display usually leans toward S&M, but that's misleading. If you're brave enough to enter and not put off by the somewhat shabby space, you'll find decadent Euro-chic party clothes that won't rob you of your last cent. **Best Find: Chiffon beaded dress $369.**

· *Nylon suit pants $295*

· **Charles David · Jean Paul Gaultier · Manigance**
· **MLC · Nora Attalia · Tark · Tempo · Via Spiga**

☺ M-Sun 11-8
Store credit or exchange w/in 7 dayst w/ receipt.

| B | B- | B | 3 |

F by Fortuna Valentino
422 West Broadway   (Prince/Spring)   212-941-5811

Is that F as in Fabulous? The shoes and bags in animal prints and crazy colors and styles are a bit on the wild side. If pony hair is not your thing, then check out the wire-frame bags covered in smooth, colorful stones. But nothing here is for the shy or the economically challenged.

· *Pony-hair zebra print ankle boots $490*

· **F by Fortuna Valentino**

☺ M-Sun 11-7
Store credit w/in 7days w/ receipt.

| C+ | B+ | A- | 3 |

René Lezard
417 West Broadway   (Prince/Spring)   212-274-0700

This icy-cool store carries a very upscale modern collection of day wear. Great for successful working women who want to update their wardrobes with future classics. **Best Find: Double-faced hand-made cashmere jacket $1395.**

· *Nylon/wool cocktail dress $465*

· **René Lezard**

☺ M-Sat 11-7, Sun 12-6
Store credit w/in 10 days w/ receipt.

| A- | A- | A | 3 |

Diesel Style Lab
416 West Broadway   (Prince/Spring)   212-343-3863

Diesel Style Lab is a more futuristic version of its parent company that modernizes simple classic designs to downtown specifications. Great chunky sweaters for winter and (of course) pants; the latter make the thin look even more so and come in nylon and other parachute-like materials. **Best Find: mohair cardigan with tie closures $95**.

· *nylon/lycra pants $245*

· **Diesel Style Lab**

⌚ M-F 11-8, Sat 11-9, Sun 11-7
Refund w/in 21 days w/ receipt. Store credit otherwise.

C+ | B- | A- |

Max Studio
415 West Broadway   (Prince/Spring)   212-941-1141

This store appeals to working women who like the prices reasonable and the clothes stylish but not startling. Max carries garments from crepe black suits to beaded cocktail dresses and is always dependable for knits and hip office wear.

· *Silk organza beaded skirt $158*

· **Max Studio**

⌚ M-Th 11-7, F-Sat 11-8, Sun 12-6
Refund w/in 14 days w/ tags and receipt.
Sale items final.

B | B+ | B+ |

Paracelso
414 West Broadway   (Prince/Spring)   212-966-4232

This store is a trip. The space looks as if it was hit by a cyclone, and the adorable owner, with blue eyebrows and green dots in place of blush, looks more like a warrior then the proprietor of this delightful boutique. Paracelso carries wonderfully unique scarves, dresses and evening bags that are so inexpensive you'll want to stock up.

· *Black beaded-mesh dress $99*

· **N/A**

⌚ M-Sun 12:30-6:30
Store credit w/in 30 days.

B+ | C- | B+ |

Otto Tootsi Plohound
413 West Broadway   (Prince/Spring)   212-925-8931

Soho day-trippers consider this long-time avant-garde shoe store a downtown monument. Long before others were bold enough to carry unusual shoes, Otto-Tootsi was packing them into its spacious, whimsically-designed boutique.

· *Otto-Tootsi Plohound leather ankle-boots $217*

· **Costume National · Duccio Del Duca · Florence Girardier**
· **Freelance · Giancarlo Paoli · Gianni Bravo**
· **Henne · Jean-Michel Cazabat · Josephine · Miu Miu**
· **Otto Tootsi Plohound · Prada · Voyage · Who's**

⌚ M-F 11:30-7:30, Sat 11-8, Sun 12-7
Exchange w/in 10 days w/ receipt.

B+ | A | A- |

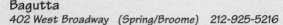

WEST BROADWAY

Country Road
411 West Broadway   (Prince/Spring)   212-343-9544

This store is ideal for working women or mothers who want a dependable selection. From time to time, though, this very down-home store produces a very cool must-have—such as a perfectly cut leather jacket—so hipsters might find it's worth the occasional look-see.

· *Suit separates, jacket $248, pants $148*

· **Country Road**

☺ M-Sat 10-8, Sun 12-6
Refund w/in 14 days w/ tags and receipt.
Store credit w/outut.

B+ | B+ | B | **2** 🐷

Bagutta
402 West Broadway (Spring/Broome) 212-925-5216

This high-priced, upscale boutique is a fashion landmark in Soho and brings European high fashion to Manhattan. Bagutta has always carried eccentric, cutting-edge designers who are about to break through into the fashion elite, and it serves customers who are willing to pay the price to stay on the crest of the fashion wave. The selection is in impeccable taste, ranging from simple beaded cardigans to mermaid-style polka-dot chiffon dresses. **Best Find: Julien MacDonald floor-length dress $3650.**

· *Anna Molinari cardigan $360*

· **Alessandro Dell' Acqua · Alexander McQueen**
· **Ann Demeulemeester · Anna Molinari · Antonio Berardi**
· **Blumarine · Chlöe · Christian Dior · Colette Dinnigan**
· **Dolce & Gabbana · Elspeth Gibson · Jean Paul Gaultier**
· **John Galliano · Julian MacDonald · Marni · Martin Kidman**
· **Matthew Williamson · Missoni · Narciso Rodriguez**
· **Olivier Theyskens**

☺ M-Sat 11-7, Sun 12-6:30
Store credit anytime with receipt.

B | A | A | **4** 🐷

Chuckies
399 West Broadway   (Spring/Broome)   212-343-1717

This shoe boutique carries a good selection of popular European brands suitable for the most fashion-forward feet. Though the Upper East Side boutique displays the merchandise in a more enticing manner, this location always has stylish footwear in stock and is excellent for casual boots and shoes in a variety of colors and leathers.

· *Chuckies ankle boots $235*

· **Alberto Guardini · Casadei · Chuckies · Cynthia Rowley**
· **David Ackerman · Ernesto Esposito · Jimmy Choo**
· **L'Autre Chose · Le Silla · Miu Miu · Moda Italia · Patrick Cox**
· **Pollini · Prada Sport · Sergio Rossi · Studio Pollini**

☺ M-Th 11-7:30, Sat 11-8, Sun 12-7:30
Store credit w/in 14 days w/ receipt.

C- | B+ | A | **3** 🐷

Eileen Fisher
395 West Broadway (Spring/Broome) 212-431-4567

These unassuming clothes are not for those who want to make a fashion statement, but women who prefer a low-key look will find jackets, wide-leg pants and occasional dress-up clothes in comfortable knits and muted tones.

· *Velvet camisole dress $188*

· **Eileen Fisher**

☺ M-Th 11-7, F-Sat 11-8, Sun 12-6
Store credit or exchange w/in 14 days w/ receipt.
Sale items final.

B- | **B+** | **A-** |

Via Spiga
390 West Broadway (Spring/Broome) 212-431-7007

The selection here is always stylish and reasonably priced, and best of all, generally comfortable. Classics like loafers are reinvented in new colors, while Prada-esque wedge sandals and flip-flops pay homage to youthful trends.

· *High-heeled Mary Janes $160*

· **Via Spiga**

☺ M-Sat 11-7, Sun 12-6
Refund w/in 7 days w/ receipt. Store credit w/in 14 days.

B+ | **B+** | **A-** |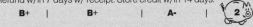

Hotel Venus
382 West Broadway (Spring/Broome) 212-966-4066

Hotel Venus is definitely not of this world. Patricia Field's second store is as fabulous and fun as her first. Wild women will find everything from Hello Kitty trinkets to rock-and-roll clothing to outrageous wigs and make-up. **Best Find: Shredded 1970s T-shirt $50.**

· *Luxe cords $78*

· **Ann Hitchcock · Carla Dawn Behrle · Cesar Arellanes · Clutch · David Dalrymple · Deviations · Hysteric Glamour · Juicy Couture · Liz Collins · Lotta · Lucky Wang · Luxe · Michael & Mushi · Miss Sixty · Oh! Ya · Playboy · Red Tape · Sergio Velente · Serious · Syren · Tripp · Velucci**

☺ M-Sun 11-8
10 day store credit, except on accessories & sale items.

B+ | **C+** | **B-** |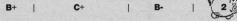

Polo Sport
381 West Broadway (Spring/Broome) 212-625-1660

Even the most devoted urbanites will long for the outdoors when they enter this Soho boutique. The atmosphere is faux ski lodge (though the habitues look more like fashion models than ski bunnies). Pick up a piece or two and you'll be transported, however briefly, out of the concrete canyons of the city.

· *Nubuck suede pants $500*

· **Polo Ralph Lauren · Polo Sport · Ralph Lauren Collection · Ralph Lauren Vintage · RLX**

☺ M-Sat 12-9, Sun 12-6
Refund w/in 30 days w/ receipt.
Store credit w/out receipt.

C+ | **A-** | **A-** |

WEST BROADWAY

Anthropologie
375 West Broadway   (Spring/Broome)   212-343-7070

This wonderful boutique is an improvement on its parent company, Urban Outfitters. Anthropologie combines popular styles with ethnically-inspired prints and fabrics. An example: colorful skirts and tops with embroidery or velvet trim. Look for the store's fantastic collection of home furnishings, organized according to the country whose traditions inspired them or from which they were imported. **Best Find: Ilia A-line suede skirt $298.**

· *Angora/lambswool sweater $58*

- **ABS · Ann Friday · Anthropologie · Buffalo**
- **CC Outlaw · Co-op · Curiositees · Double A**
- **Easel · F.r.e.e. · Fortune Favors A Prepared Mind**
- **Free People · Hype · Illia · In the Know · Leopold**
- **Liquid · Lulu Lame · Maxou · Michael Stars**
- **Mini by X-Large · New York Based · Only Hearts**
- **Phillip Chi · Plenty · Sanctuary · Sleeping on the Snow**
- **Sweat Pea · Sweet Romeo · Tease Tees · Tessuto**
- **Tracy Reese · Work Order**

☺ M-Sat 11-8, Sun 11-6
Refund w/ receipt.
Store credit w/out receipt.

| C+ | A | B | |

What Comes Around Goes Around
351 West Broadway   (Broome/Grand)   212-343-9303

The store's name refers not to karmic retribution, but to the clothes it carries, which are some of the best vintage duds in Manhattan. You'll find Levi's, Pucci dresses from the 70s, and worn-in leather jackets, among other items. Unfortunately, what went around the first time is almost as expensive this time. **Best Find: Silk Pucci skirt $425.**

· *Cashmere v-neck sweater $75*

· **N/A**

☺ M-Th 11-8, F-Sat 11-12, Sun 12-7
Store credit w/in 7 days w/ receipt.

| C+ | B+ | B- | |

Manrico
140 Wooster St.   (Houston/Prince)   212-253-9877

This unremarkable Soho boutique pales in comparison to its uptown sister. Though grand in scale, the giant space makes the limited selection of simple modern cashmere sweaters seem insignificant. The fitted sweaters are a bit more stylized than most and best for the younger shopper—though younger shoppers don't seem to be the demographic most likely to fork over $600 for a short-sleeve sweater.

· *Open v-neck cashmere short-sleeve sweater with collar $640*

· **Manrico**

☺ M-Sat 11-7, Sun 12-6
Store credit anytime w/ receipt.

| C+ | B- | A | |

Pleats Please
128 Wooster St.   (@ Prince)   212-226-3600

Issey Miyake's bridge line is still avant-garde to the max. The crisp, narrowly pleated fabrics are cut in shapes that recall lampshades or futuristic samurai outfits, and some of the pieces feature detailing like cigarette burns. If you're among Issey Miyake's following, you already know who you are. Otherwise, stop in here for a look, but when it comes to buying, the phrase to remember is "Pleats, no thank you."

· *Pleated print dress $295*

· **Pleats Please**

🕐 M-S 11-7, Sun 11-6
Store credit w/in 7 days w/ receipt.

B | B | A- |

Malo
125 Wooster St.   (Prince/Spring)   212-941-7444

One of the finest cashmere shops New York has to offer. If you find the expensive cashmere sweaters prohibitive, head downstairs for the timeless and fashionable line of ready-to-wear clothing. Pick up one of the sleek candles for home decoration while you're at it. Expect to be followed by the suspicious sales staff, who guard their pricey clothing as if it were gold bullion.

· *Cashmere twin-set ("2 for the price of 1") $726*

· **Malo**

🕐 M-Sat 11-7, Sun 12-6
Store credit w/in 10 days w/ receipt.

B- | B+ | A+ |

Todd Oldham
123 Wooster St.   (Prince/Spring)   212-219-3531

Color-phobic shoppers should steer clear of this shop, where 60s acid haze meets 90s kitsch. Totally unlike Todd Oldham's discontinued collection, this line of clothing is heavy on T-shirts, jeans, and busy prints. These clothes are young, playful, and for weekends only. **Best Find: Orange cotton sweater $80**.

· *Jeans $45*

· **Todd Oldham**

🕐 M-Sat 11-7, Sun 12-7
Store credit w/in 10 days.

B | B | B+ |

M-A-G
120 Wooster St.   (Prince/Spring)   212-965-1898

Though working itself may be stressful and annoying, buying clothes for work shouldn't have to be. Not only will you find the womb-like atmosphere of M.A.G and the background noise of falling water relaxing, but the luxuriously soft wools and cashmere sweaters and pants will make you feel pampered even when you're pulling them on Monday at 6 a.m. **Best Find: Cashmere pants $220**.

· *Cashmere hooded shawl $422*

· **M-A-G**

🕐 M-Sat 11-7:30, Sun 12-6
Store credit w/in 10 days w/ receipt.

B | B | A- |

WOOSTER STREET

Prada Sport
116 Wooster St.   (Prince/Spring)   212-925-2221

In a word: tragic. In two words: fashion victim. Every great love affair has its ups and downs, and for those who swooned over Prada, Prada Sport is a major trough. Don't be misled by the stylish parent label. The goods here are simply weird and unflattering, not to mention outrageously expensive for "sportswear."

· *Wool sweater with nylon panels and belt $660*

· **Prada Sport**

☉ M-Sat 11-7, Sun 12-6
Refund w/in 10 days. Store credit afterward.

| C | B- | A | |

Barbara Bui
115 Wooster St.   (Prince/Spring)   212-625-1938

Barbara Bui previously catered to the sophisticated middle-aged woman, but it seems that being in Soho has led her astray. Formerly noted for her classic styling (particularly in suits), she seems to have been affected by minimalist downtown sensibilities. It's not clear who is the intended customer for this unimaginative store, but she better have deep pockets. **Best Find: Nylon techo-garb pants $350.**

· *Wool suit-jacket $830, pants $380*

· **Barbara Bui**

☉ M-Sat 11-7, Sun 12-6
Store credit w/in 10 days w/ receipt.

| B- | A- | A | |

Cynthia Rowley
112 Wooster St.   (Prince/Spring)   212-334-1144

Think June Cleaver in the 21st century. This boutique returns to the structured, prim and proper dress of bygone years and makes conservative seem sexy. Whether it's a simple frill or a glimmering sparkle, Rowley is always updating styles of the past with deceptively simple details. Her use of color is never ostentatious and will make any prom-goer or feminine twenty-something feel like a princess. **Best Find: Flat leopard bag $145.**

· *Ankle-length silk gown $440*

· **Cynthia Rowley**

☉ M-W 11-7, Th-F 11-8, Sat 11-7, Sun 12-6
Store credit w/in 7 days. Sale items final.

| B | A- | A- | 3 |

Costume National
108 Wooster St.   (Prince/Spring)   212-431-1530

Reminiscent of the milk bar in "A Clockwork Orange," Costume National is the kind of store in which to find outrageous super-chic separates such as leather halters, purple ankle boots, and green snakeskin motorcycle jackets. The best accessory for these clothes: a super-tight body. **Best Find: Green python jacket $2783.**

· *Peach leather turtleneck halter $496*

· **Costume National**

☉ M-Sat 11-7, Sun 12-6
Store credit w/in 10 days w/ receipt.

| B | A | A | 4 |

Patagonia
101 Wooster St.   *(Prince/Spring)*   212-343-1776

Nothing is as soft, warm, and useful as a fleece from Patagonia. Unless you're a hard-core outdoor type, one is probably all you'll need, since they last a lifetime.

· *R3 zipper fleece $134*

· **Patagonia**

🕒 M-Sat 11-8, Sun 12-7
Refund w/ tags & receipt.

B- | **C+** | **A-** | *3*

Laundry by Shelli Segal
97 Wooster St.   *(Prince/Spring)*   212-334-9433

The modern atmosphere of her boutique somehow detracts from Segal's pretty, sophisticated, and reasonably-priced clothing. However, the line is still fabulous, particularly in winter, so sit your husband down in a plush white chair and let him watch you try on various outfits, with the help of the attentive sales people. **Best Find: Wool/cashmere blend eyelet capri pants $148**.

· *Beaded suit-jacket $278; pants $188; skirt $148*

· **Laundry**

🕒 M-Sat 11-7, Sun 12-6
Store credit w/in 7 days w/ receipt.

B+ | **B+** | **A-** | *3*

Morgane Le Fay
67 Wooster St.   *(Spring/Broome)*   212-219-7672

When you enter Morgane Le Fay, you may feel that you're in a dreamscape. Elegant, modern clothing hangs suspended from the heavens in this cavernous space, and the sound of opera arias fills the air. Don't let the pretentious attitudes of the sales staff jar you out of the otherwise blissful experience of shopping here, and pick up a filmy, layered full-skirted dress or a delicate, streamlined coat. **Best Find: Red velvet gown $1600**.

· *Light wool ankle-length skirt with satin trim at waist $340*

· **Morgane Le Fay**

🕒 M-Sun 11-7
Store credit w/in 7 days w/ receipt.

D+ | **A+** | **A** | *4*

Steven Alan
60 Wooster St.   *Spring/Broome)*   212-334-6354

The homey and intimate atmosphere of this boutique will make you feel like you're at a friend's apartment trying on her things. Lucky friend! Steven Alan packs in the ultra-cool labels, and you're sure to find plenty of items to covet.

· *Earl jeans $107*

· **6 by Martin Margiela · Built by Wendy · Holmes & Lyell · Intensity · Katayone Adeli · Lascaux · Le Havlin Piro · Mint · Noodle · P.A.K. · Paul & Joe · Pauline · Petit Bateau · Rebecca Dannenberg · Red Tape · Ripcosa · Rubin Chapelle · Sally Penn · SVO · TTMX · Ulla Johnson · United Bamboo · Vanessa Bruno · Yoon**

🕒 M-Sat 11-7, Sun 12-7
Store credit w/in 7 days w/ receipt.

B | **B+** | **A-** | *3*

WOOSTER STREET

Riva Mirasager
28 Wooster St. (@ Grand) 212-334-3860

If you want to feel like Rita Hayworth as Gilda or any other 1940s vixen, check out this slinky collection of dresses and suits. The stark white space with huge columns is a fitting setting for this dramatic line, where the tall and lean can find anything from an elegant evening look to a non-traditional wedding dress.

· *Long-sleeve matte jersey bias-cut gown $1000*

· **Riva Mirasager**

☺ M-F 12-7, Sat 11-7:30, Sun 12-6
All sales final.

| A- | A | A- | |

Louis Vuitton
116 Greene St. (Prince/Spring) 212-274-9090

Some stores have a reputation to uphold, and Louis Vuitton takes its reputation seriously. Don't expect to be embraced with open arms unless you wear your Platinum Card on your sleeve. These beautiful bags and accessories have always had cachet, but a few seasons ago Louis Vuitton's clothing became screamingly chic.

· *Dress $1550*

· **Louis Vuitton**

☺ M-Sat 11-7, Sun 12-6
Refund w/in 15 days w/ receipt.
Store credit otherwise.

| D | A | A+ | |

Joseph (pant store)
115 Greene St. (Prince/Spring) 212-343-7071

The demand for these sexy slender pants was so great that Joseph had to open a store dedicated to the fashion favorite. The small store houses an infinite supply of the chicest pants in town. Alas: if you haven't got the legs of a fashion model, you may have trouble sliding them on. **Best Find: Red velour stretch pants $299**.

· *Wool pants $299*

· **Joseph**

☺ M-Sat 11-7:30, Sun 12-6
Store credit w/ receipt.

| C | B- | A- |  |

Anna Sui
113 Greene St. (Prince/Spring) 212-941-8406

Glam it up at Anna Sui, where the Addams Family meets rock-and-roll. From feathered boas to floor-length shearling coats with dyed edges, the clothing is geared to the hip and fashionably bold. **Best Find: Mohair boas $180**.

· *Fox-trimmed suede coat $1455*

· **Anna Sui**

☺ M-Sat 11:30-7, Sun 12-6
Store credit w/in 7 days. Accessories final.

| B+ | A | A | |

SOHO

Jill Stuart
100 Greene St. *(Prince/Spring)* *212-343-2300*

Having strayed from the innocent girlishness of her past, Stuart has spent recent years exploring her edgier side. Her clothes have a downtown cool appeal that her earlier dresses lacked. Don't mourn the loss—several others have copied her with competence, and her new style is a welcome change for the young and hip. **Best Find: Wool coat with leather tie $560.**

· *Hot pink embroidered sling-back shoes $275*

· **Jill Stuart**

☺ M-Sat 11-7, Sun 12-6
Exchange w/in 7 days w/ receipt. Shoe sales final.

| B- | A | A- | |

Vivienne Tam
99 Greene St. *(Prince/Spring)* *212-966-2398*

Crazy colors, kitschy patterns, and stretchy gauze are the hallmarks of Tam's colorful boutique. This designer's flagship store offers her own line of clothes for the young at heart. Warning: spare tires and love handles not welcome. **Best Find: Green beaded knee-length dress $1295.**

· *Beaded rayon/lycra skirt $430*

· **Vivienne Tam**

☺ M-F 11-7, Sat 11:30-7:30, Sun 12-7
Store credit w/in 7 days w/ receipt.

| B | A- | A- | |

Kirna Zabête
96 Greene St. *(Prince/Spring)* *212-941-9656*

The latest "it" store in Soho, this boutique distinguishes itself by offering the oddest, most expensive fashion pieces of the next moment. For the most part, the clothes are impractical, but the chic accessories are a find. Even if you have no intention of buying, the two-story space is worth visiting for the educational value alone: each of the forty-odd designers' clothes are displayed on the racks with helpful little name-tags. **Best Find: Paul Smith sea-green velvet pants $385.**

· *Wool pants $495*

· **Alain Tondowski · Andrew GN · Ann-Louise Roswald**
· **Antoni & Alison · Anya Hindmark · Balenciaga**
· **Boyd · Bruce · Clements Ribeiro · E. Vil · Eley Kishmoto**
· **Grab & Mac · Hussein Chalayan · Jenny Udale**
· **Jurgi Persoons · Jo Gordon · Lambertson Truex**
· **Louison · Lulu Guinness · Madame à Paris**
· **Martine Sitbon · Mathew Williamson · Megan Park**
· **Mira · Mischa Lampert · Olivier Theyskens · Paul Smith**
· **Rick Owens · Rodolphe Menudier · Rubin Chapelle**
· **Susan Cianciolo · Thimister · Tony Valentino · Wink**

☺ M-Sat 11-7, Sun 12-6
Store credit w/in 30 days.

| B- | A+ | A | |

GREENE STREET

Anne Fontaine
93 Greene St. *(Prince/Spring)* 212-343-3154

This shop proves once again that "simple" doesn't necessarily mean "plain." Anne Fontaine's wide selection of beautifully tailored French white shirts are luxuriously soft and come different styles and cuts to provide countless variations on an old favorite.

· *White cotton shirts $135-$180*

· **Anne Fontaine**

☺ M-Sat 11-7, Sun 12-6
Refund w/in 21 days.

B	A	A	

Tehen
91 Greene St. *(Prince/Spring)* 212-925-4788

The roomy styles and generous fabrics of Tehen's house line will look stylish on most body types. Like the understated and relaxed store, the clothing exudes a no-effort chic. The store's specialty knits include spacious sweater coats, turtlenecks, and skirts that leave at least some aspects of a woman's figure to the imagination.

· *Ankle-length skirt $300*

· **Tehen**

☺ M-Sat 11-7, Sun 12-6
Store credit w/in 30 days w/ receipt.

B+	A-	A	

Helmut Lang
80 Greene St. *(Spring/Broome)* 212-925-7214

Helmut Lang's severe, innovative clothes are sexy in a bad-girl, post-apocalyptic kind of way, but they're definitely not for everybody. Silver leather motorcycle pants are a typical item—some women will swoon, and others will run for their lives. But beyond all the Mad Max trappings, one thing cannot be denied: nobody cuts a pair of pants like Helmut Lang. **Best Find: Cashmere cream-colored scarf $310**.

· *Vintage-look jeans $200*

· **Helmut Lang**

☺ M-Sat 11-7, Sun 12-6
10 days store credit or exchange.

C	A-	A+	

Vivienne Westwood
71 Greene St. *(Spring/Broome)* 212-334-5200

Vivienne Westwood still makes her classic punk-rock kilts in lengths so short that they redefine the term "mini." There's nothing punk about her prices, though. The bustles and jackets that comprise Westwood's trademark Edwardian-schoolgirl-gone-bad look are marvels of tailoring skill. **Best Find: Knee-length olive-green suede dress $1700**.

· *Red label suit jacket $700*

· **Vivienne Westwood**

☺ M-Sat 11-7, Sun 12-6
Store credit w/in 30 days w/ receipt. Sale items final.

C+	A	A+	

SOHO

Plein Sud
70 Greene St.   *(Spring/Broome)*   212-431-8800

Plein Sud is French ready-to-wear at its finest. The elegant decor in the shop compliments the chic collection, styled in luxurious fabrics. Sophisticated women of means will be seriously tempted by leathers and furs that blur the distinction between day wear and evening wear.

· *Jersey pants $396*

· **Plein Sud**

☉ M-Sat 11-7, Sun 12-6
Store credit w/in 8 days w/ receipt.

| B+ | A | A+ | |

Ventilo
69 Greene St.   *(Spring/Broome)*   212-625-3660

With stark white walls and dark wood floors, Ventilo's enormous retail space is more impressive than its clothing. The atmosphere is perfect for housing the eclectic collection of French-and-Asian influenced pieces. **Best Find: Hand embroidered ankle-length Indian wedding skirt $1500.**

· *Wool pants $125*

· **Ventilo**

☉ M-Sat 11-7, Sun 12-6
Store credit w/in 10 days. Evening wear sales final.

| A- | A- | A- | |

Daang Goodman
68 Greene St.   *(Spring/Broome)*   212-226-7465

Daang Goodman's purple floor-length faux-fur coats, geometric suits, and other artsy confections will land you on the "Don't" pages of the fashion magazines, but you can comfort yourself with the thought that you are so cool that no one—NO ONE—can understand your fashion sense.

· *Mid-calf black nylon coat with oversized pockets $675.*

· **5351** · **Daang Goodman** · **E-play** · **Fornarina**
· **Mandarina Duck** · **Petit Bateau** · **Tripp**

☉ M-W 11-7, Th-Sat 11-7:30, Sun 12-6
Store credit w/in 7 days w/ receipt.

| C+ | B- | B | |

Keiko
62 Greene St.   *(Spring/Broome)*   212-226-6051

Unless you're a supermodel, shopping for a bathing suit has to be one of life's most traumatic experiences. Suits that fit mannequins beautifully have a way of gapping and stretching in all the wrong places when real women put them on. Here, you can mix and match vibrantly-colored tops and bottoms of unequal size until you've found that elusive "perfect" fit.

· *Basic bikini $110*

· **Keiko**

☉ M-F 11-6, Sat 12-6, Sun 1-6
Exchange w/in 15 days w/ receipt.

| A | A- | A- | |

service | presentation | quality | expense

GREENE STREET

Su-Zen
17 Greene St. *(Grand/Canal)* 212-925-3744

You'll want to move right into this gorgeous store. Here's where baby boomers shopping in Soho with their size-two daughters can find a little something that's more their style. The clothes come in "normal"—west of the Hudson—sizes, which makes up for the fact that they're sometimes more comfortable than chic.

· *Velour pullover sweater $420*

· **Su-Zen**

☺ M-Sat 11-7, Sun 12-6
Exchange w/in 7 dats w/ receipt.

A- | A- | A- |

Marc Jacobs
163 Mercer St. *(Houston/Prince)* 212-343-1490

Three words: to die for. There is no item in this designer's collection that any shopper in her right mind wouldn't want. The timeless style and exceptional quality are so utterly enticing that you'd probably sell your soul to the devil for even a single skirt. **Best Find: Tuxedo-striped denim pants $650.**

· *Wool knee-length skirt $990*

· **Marc Jacobs**

☺ M-Sat 11-7, Sun 12-6
Store credit w/in 7 days w/ receipt.

B- | A- | A+ |

Tocca
161 Mercer St. *(Houston/Prince)* 212-343-3912

Tocca made its name with sweet little eyelet slip dresses, and the look is still ultimate girly girl. The clothes are structured, delicate, and easy on the eye. If you have no desire to play Lolita yourself, buy a child's-size version of these numbers for a little one. Don't forget to check out the dreamy bedding, which can make any room into a fairy-tale setting.

· *Silk embroidered knee-length skirt $189*

· **Tocca**

☺ M-Sat 11-7, Sun 12-6
Store credit w/in 10 days w/ receipt.

C+ | C | A- |

A.P.C.
131 Mercer St. *(Prince/Spring)* 212-966-9685

An upscale Club Monaco, A.P.C. is known for stylish urban staples and a customer base that is limited to waif-ish women. Its low-rider winter cords and summer khakis tend to come in neutral tones, though some colors do pop up seasonally. **Best Find: Wool duffel jacket $370.**

· *100% cotton shirt $100*

· **A.P.C.**

☺ M-Sat 11-7, Sun 12-6
Store credit w/in 7 days w/ receipt.

C+ | B+ | A- |

service | presentation | quality | expense

Shin Choi/Coleridge
119 Mercer St.   (Prince/Spring)   212-625-9202

Shin Choi—formerly known as Coleridge—offers a beautiful line of day wear that is both elegant and simple. The tailored coats, shift dresses, and funnel-neck shirts are enticing in a range of luxurious fabrics and soft colors. You can assemble a distinctive yet pulled-together wardrobe here with very little effort. **Best Find: Red cashmere knee-length coat $775.**

· *Funnel-neck baby alpaca top $354*

· **Shin Choi/Coleridge**

☺ M-Sat 11-7
Store credit w/in 10 days w/ receipt.

A-	A-	A	

Yvone Christa
107 Mercer St.   (Prince/Spring)   212-965-1001

Think small. This teeny store is so unassuming you might pass it by. Do not. Inside Yvone Christa, you'll find a great selection of well-priced snakeskin handbags in several shapes and sizes and a variety of hot colors. The wonderful satin evening bags with floral trim are perfect for a night on the town. **Best Find: Green snakeskin baguette-style bag $185.**

· *Oriental-style evening bag $95*

· **NY Look · Yvone Christa**

☺ M-F 12-8, Sat 1-8, Sun 2-8
Store credit w/in 14 days w/ receipt.

A-	B+	B+	

Product
71 Mercer St.   (Spring/Broome)   212-274-1494

This line was the promising equivalent to Tahari's very popular Theory label. While Product's hype has diminished, the line remains a favorite, particularly with younger women. The small boutique, hidden away in Soho, features an edgier line of stylish clothing. Product always uses interesting fabrics, though the cuts are on the small side. **Best Find: Charcoal ankle-length knit skirt $125.**

· *Nylon/spandex fitted pants $125*

· **Product**

☺ M-Sat 11-7, Sun 12-6
Store credit w/in 5 days.

B	B-	B+	

Marianne Novobotsky
65 Mercer St.   (@ Broome)   212-431-4120

If you don't want to wear black to a black-tie affair, you'll find an alternative at this couture boutique. The appealing floor samples of colorful silk-taffeta ballroom skirts and matching corsets, gowns and jackets will appeal to the sophisticated woman who enjoys classic styles with a little pizzazz.

· *Bustier $480*

· **Marianne Novobotsky**

☺ M-Sun 12-7, Sat 11-5 or appt.
All sales final.

B+	B+	A	

BROADWAY

A/X Armani Exchange
568 Broadway   (Houston/Prince)   **212-431-6000**

The lowest-quality level on the Armani totem pole, A/X Armani Exchange attempts to target the younger set by dazzling it with boring basics like jeans and white button-down shirts.

· *Cotton/polyester skirt $78*

· **A/X Armani Exchange**

☺ M-Sat 10-8, Sun 11-7
Refund w/in 30 days w/ receipt. Exchange w/out receipt.

B	B	B+

Juno
550 Broadway   (Prince/Spring)   **212-925-6415**

Fashion slaves will be happy to know that they're investing in durable shoes—even if they won't be wearing them next year. And if your footsies are as big as Tootsie's, you will be happy to know that Juno stocks a wide selection of larger sizes.

· *Juno Mary Jane with pony strap $185*

· **Debut · Everyone · Exe · Jo Ghost · Juno · L'Autre Chose**
· **Roberto de Carlo · Trussardo · Vic Matie · Zaza**

☺ M-F 10:30-8, Sat 10:30-8:30, Sun 11:30-8
Store credit w/in 7 days w/ receipt.

C+	B+	B+

Mystique Boutique
547 Broadway   (Prince/Spring)   **212-274-0645**

Warning: High Cheese Factor. It takes a hot body and lot of natural style to avoid looking cheap and sleazy in the clothes you'll find here. Watch the prices, too: as Bette Midler once said, it costs a lot of money to look this cheap. **Best Find: Leopard print fuzzy fishtail skirt $60**.

· *Polyester print shirt $70*

· **Cheap Thrill · G.O.D. · Lip Service · Mystique Boutique**
· **Paris Blues · Shendel · Z. Cavaricci**

☺ M-Sat 10-9, Sun, 11-8
Store credit w/in 7 days w/ receipt.

D+	C-	C-

Heun
543 Broadway   (Prince/Spring)   **212-625-2560**

This stark, spacious store carries a trendy selection of lesser-known designers. The clothes are good for working twenty- or thirtysomethings whose sensibilities are a little left of center. Pick up an orange-and- blue cashmere sweater with ties on the sleeves, pair it with plain black pants, and complete the outfit with shoes from the large selection in the back of the store. **Best Find: Rose D wool/cashmere sweater with sleeve ties $180**.

· *Viscose/nylon stretch top $145*

· **Bertelli · Dalmata · Divina · Enjoy · Ensemble · Heun**
· **Jay Coleman · Kitoshi · Lorella Braglia · Loretta Di Lorenzo**
· **Okosi · Rose D · Zooi**

☺ M-Sat 10:30-8, Sun 11-8
Store credit or exchange w/in 7 days w/ receipt.

C+	B+	A-

Scoop
532 Broadway   (Prince/Spring)   212-925-2886

Scoop carries the most feminine clothes without being a slave to fashion. Color is the key in this store, where the clothes are a combination of Upper East Side sophistication and downtown cool with an ethnic influence.

· *Earl suede jeans $520*

· **Blumarine** · **Chaiken & Capone** · **Daryl K** · **Diane Von Furstenberg** · **Earl Jeans** · **Easel** · **Ghost** · **Inca** · **Jimmy Choo** · **Katayone Adeli** · **Petit Bateau** · **Shoshanna** · **Theory** · **William B**

☺ M-Sat 11-8, Sun 11-7
Store credit w/in 14 days.

C+ | A | A |

Sharagano
529 Broadway   (Prince/Spring)   212-941-7086

The underlying theme here: the best things come in small packages. A tiny but perfectly chosen selection of cool styles that range from wool and fringed sweaters to classic black pants sets this shop apart. The quality is acceptable and prices are reasonable. **Best Find: Acrylic/polyester fringed poncho $138.**

· *Cotton/lycra pants $108*

· **Sharagano**

☺ M-W 11-8, Th-Sat 10-9, Sun 11-8
10 day exchange; Store credit w/ receipt.

B- | B- | B+ |

David Aaron
529 Broadway   (Prince/Spring)   212-431-6022

David Aaron has his ear to the ground for the trendy, so this is where you'll find early knockoffs of designs from Prada and other high-end names. His original designs are as trendy and upscale, yet more affordable than those they mimic.

· *Pony-hair loafers $89*

· **David Aaron**

☺ M-F 11-8, Sat 11-8:30, Sun 11-7:30
Refund w/in 14 days w/ receipt.

C+ | B | B |

Zabari
506 Broadway   (Spring/Broome)   212-431-7502

Like the large, unfinished space it inhabits, the merchandise in Zabari seems to exist in limbo. It's somewhere between cheesy/trendy and cool/up-and-coming designers. Shopping here can be an adventure—you might find anything from a patchwork miniskirt to a striking wool coat. **Best Find: Bubu ankle-length spring skirt $189.**

· *Suede floor-length gowns by Zabari $595*

· **120%** · **Alice & Trixie** · **Anna Kuan** · **Bubu** · **Capucine Puerari** · **Demoo Parkchoon Moo** · **Free Follies** · **Lotta** · **Michael Greening** · **Pin up** · **QUD** · **Rebeccallison** · **Rojas** · **Sweet Romeo** · **Tooke** · **Zabari**

☺ M-F 11-8, Sat-Sun 11-9
Store credit w/in 7 days w/ tags and receipt.

B | B+ | B+ |

B R O A D W A Y

Canal Jeans
504 Broadway   (Spring/Broome)   212-226-1130

Canal Jeans gained notoriety for being a treasure chest of cheap second-hand clothes. Though it still carries an extensive collection of used merchandise, it has upgraded considerably and now offers a tremendous range of favorite basics from both the past and the present.

· *Sergio Valente Jeans $74*

· **Bubble Gum · Calvin Klein · CK Calvin Klein**
· **Dickies · Dollhouse · French Connection · Groggy**
· **Kenneth Cole Reaction · Levi's · Lip Service**
· **Polo Jeans · Schott Brothers · Sergio Valente**
· **Serious · Soda Blu · Todd Oldham · Tripp · Union Bay**

☺ M-Sun 9:30-9
Store credit w/ tags and receipt w/in 7 days.

C+ | C+ | C+ |

Old Navy
503 Broadway   (Spring/Broome)   212-226-0838

This is the hipper, cooler, younger—and, very key—less expensive version of its parent company, The Gap. The clothes will most appeal to pre-teens and teeny-boppers, but women seeking a good selection of stylish basics may discover a new best friend in Old Navy. **Best Find: Thermal hooded T-shirt with 3/4" sleeve $16**.

· *Cords $30*

· **Old Navy**

☺ M-Sat 10-9, Sun 11-8
Refund w/in 30 days w/ receipt. Store credit otherwise.

C | C+ | B- |

Rose Ann's
495 Broadway, 7th Floor (Spring/Broome) 212-226-6066

At Rose Ann's showroom, "custom" has real pizzazz. The designer uses high-quality, unbelievably detailed fabrics also used by the major fashion houses to transform simple styles into drop-dead gorgeous gowns. Rose Ann also specializes in suits as well as cocktail dresses and pre-teen formal wear. Pass it on.

· *Evening gowns $1500-$4000*

· **Rose Ann's**

☺ By appt. only
All sales final.

A+ | B | A+ |

Alice Underground
481 Broadway   (Broome/Grand)   212-431-9067

One of the leading second-hand stores in New York, Alice Underground carries a well-organized selection of typical vintage fare. Though they're not giving anything away, you do get your money's worth. **Best Find: Beaded tops $65-$95**.

· *Levi's $25*

· **N/A**

☺ M-Sun 11-7:30
All sales final.

C+ | B+ | B- |

service | presentation | quality | expense

Yellow Rat Bastard
478 Broadway   (Broome/Grand)   212-334-2150

The immature collection of trendy "urban" clothing at this boutique runs along the line of jeans, denim tops and some teeny-bopper labels. But the best thing about Yellow Rat Bastard is still its name.

· *Sweater $46*

· **AMX** · **Diesel** · **Echo** · **Kickwear** · **P&B** · **Sample NYC**
· **Triple 5 Soul** · **UFO**

☺ M-Sat 10-9, Sun 12-8
Exchange w/in 14 days w/ tags and receipt.

    C+ | C+ | C+ |

Detour
154 Prince St.   (Thompson/W. Broadway)   212-966-3635

Ever trendy and fun, Detour's second store is stocked with a younger and more playful selection of clothes than the first. The store is filled with popular continental labels, and you'll be sure to find some great items for both work and play.

· *Orange fleece skirt $120*

· **Blue Birdy** · **M Lulu** · **Pinko** · **Poleci** · **Sweet Pea** · **Velvet**

☺ M-Sun 11-8
Store credit w/in 7 days w/ receipt.

    D | B- | A- |

Nicole Miller
134 Prince St.   (W. Broadway/Wooster)   212-343-1362

Nicole Miller has built her empire on the kitschy patterns and classic styles which define her line of elegant evening attire. Though the prints sometimes get a little too crazy, Nicole Miller remains a great resource for dress wear.

· *Satin column dress $250*

· **Nicole Miller**

☺ M-Sat 11-7, Sun 12-6
Store credit w/in 7 days w/ receipt.
Evening wear sales final.

    C+ | B+ | A- |

Phat Farm
129 Prince St.   (W. Broadway/Wooster)   212-533-PHAT

This urban street-wear shop, known for its sweatshirts and jackets, is expanding Baby Phat, its women's line, this spring. In addition to the tank tops and baby tees, Baby Phat now features a full line of sexy clothing, including dresses, skirts and pants that are sure to be eye-catchers. Also being launched is a super-sexy line of lingerie, to be carried at popular stores in addition to Phat Farm's home base.

· *Baby Phat tank-top $25*

· **Baby Phat** · **Phat Farm**

☺ M-Sat 11-7, Sun 12-6
7 days exchange or store credit w/ receipt.

    B | B+ | B |

PRINCE STREET

Rampage
127 Prince St.   (@ Wooster)   212-995-9569

Don't go on a spending rampage in this trendy boutique. Though it's a fine source for the younger set seeking cheap club-wear or party clothes, what you buy this season will become the woolly mammoth of fashion in a heartbeat. A good eye for style can find good buys, but exercise caution or you'll turn into a big hunk of cheese. **Best Find: Silk and cashmere 3/4 length v-neck sweater $48.**

· *Spandex hip-hugger pants $38*

· **Dollhouse** · **French Connection** · **Heart Moon Star**
· **Levi's** · **XOXO**

☺ M-Sat 10-8, Sun 11-7
Refund w/in 30 days w/ tag and receipt.
Manager must approve exchanges.

| C | C | C- | |

Harriet Love
126 Prince St.   (Wooster/Greene)   212-966-2280

In the heart of Soho, frumpy clothes may seem out of place, but out-of towners may feel as if they've stumbled into a familiar oasis in otherwise foreign territory. Items like beaded gloves and embroidered pashmina handbags have a wide appeal, making Harriet Love a great place for gifts. **Best Find: Orange mohair embroidered and beaded bag $187.**

· *Wool/cashmere gloves $35*

· **Bruuns Bazaar** · **Cow Girls** · **Curiositees** · **D.A.R.**
· **Grass Roots** · **Juicy Couture** · **Lilith** · **Ohm** · **Robin Richman**

☺ M-Sun 11-7
7 days store credit or exchange. Receipt preferred.

| B | C+ | B | |

Agnés B.
116-118 Prince St.   (Wooster/Greene)   212-925-4649

Agnés B. has captured simple Parisian style and brought it effortlessly to New York. Truly appropriate for a woman of any age, the store is always stylish without being "fashionable."

· *Cotton cardigan T-shirt $45*

· **Agnés B.**

☺ M-Sun 11-7
Store credit w/in 10 days.

| C+ | A- | B- | |

Miu Miu
100 Prince St.   (Greene/Mercer)   212-334-5156

Nowadays, Miu Miu, Prada's less expensive offspring, often verges on the weird and unwearable, and of late some of its offerings resemble an April Fool's joke. You can find the occasional everyday piece, such as a suede A-line skirt or wool sweater, but most of the bizarre selection screams "Miu Miu" so loudly that your individuality will be lost in the din.

· *Wool skirt $230*

· **Miu Miu**

☺ M-Sat 11-7, Sun 12-6
Store credit w/in 10 days w/ receipt.

| D | A- | A- | |

J. Crew
99 Prince St.   (@ Mercer)   212-966-2739

S O H O

Those of you who have been living in caves for the last ten years might not know that this famous catalogue retailer now has stores all over Manhattan. J. Crew offers clothes for women of every age with a variety of cuts, styles, and price points. The clothes are never boring, but they're never too trendy either. J. Crew customers really get their money's worth in terms of both style and quality.

· *Sweaters $60*

· **J. Crew**

☺ M-F 10-8, Sat 11-8, Sun 12-7
Refund w/ receipt and tags. Store credit w/out receipt.

| A- | A- | A- | |

Big Drop
174 Spring St.   (Thompson/W. Broadway)   212-966-4299

Once a Soho-only boutique, this shop predates Scoop. Big Drop carries some up-and-coming designers with big talent as well as some familiar favorites. Older twenty-somethings who aren't on a budget can find some exceptional pieces here. A wonderful collection of unique handbags helps make this shop a worthy destination.

· *Sweater dress $300*

· **6 by Martin Margiela · Big Drop · Earl Jeans**
· **Juicy Couture· Rebecca Dannenberg · Tracy Reese**
· **Urchin · Vanessa Bruno · Wayne Cooper**
· **White & Warren**

☺ M-Sat 11-8, Sun 12-7
Store credit w/in 7 days.

| C- | B | A- | |

Freelance
155 Spring St.   (W. Broadway/Wooster)   212-965-9231

In Soho, Freelance is the "it" spot for boots. The styles range from the year-round collection of chunky-heeled ankle boots to seasonal trends like this winter's snakeskin and pony hair. Everything is timelessly stylish and built to last—and that goes for the shoes, too.

· *Leather round-toed boots with chunky heel $228*

· **Freelance**

☺ M-F 11:30-7:30, Sat 11-7, Sun 12-8
Store credit w/in 10 days w/ receipt.

| C+ | A- | A- | |

Morgane Le Fay Home
151 Spring St.   (W. Broadway/Wooster)   212-925-0144

This location carries Morgan Le Fay's less expensive casual line. Layering is big, but if you can sift through the strange pieces and make yourself try them on, you may be pleasantly surprised by the merchandise. Each piece is guaranteed to add a unique touch to your wardrobe.

· *Velvet A-line skirt $180*

· **Morgane Le Fay**

☺ M-Sun 11-7
Store credit w/in 7 days w/ receipt.

| B | B | A- | |

service | presentation | quality | expense

Putumayo
147 Spring St.   (W. Broadway/Wooster)   212-966-4458

Not a hipster's haven, but an excellent resource to pick up a textile wool skirt and linen blouse. Putumayo's earthy clothing avoids frumpiness thanks to high-quality fabrics and cuts that don't simply cover bodies but actually flatter them.

· *Linen shirt $78*

· **Flax** · **Putumayo** · **White Wash**

☺ M-Sat 11-7, Sun 12-6
Refund w/in 14 days w/ tags and receipt.
Store credit w/in 30 days.

C+ | B | B+ |

Oasis
138 Spring St.   (@ Wooster)   212-219-0710

The spacious boutique boasts racks and racks of trendy clothing for the working woman who also knows how to have a good time. The labels are popular, stylish lines and there is a remarkably good balance between clothes for day and night. **Best Find: Bianca Nero rayon column dress $312.**

· *Long wool skirt $240*

· **Bianca Nero** · **Easel** · **Icon** · **Only Hearts** · **Page 3**
· **Teen Flo** · **Theory** · **Yigal Azrouel**

☺ M-Sat 11-7:30, Sun 11:30-7
Store credit w/in 7 days w/ receipt.

C+ | B+ | A- |

Institut
97 Spring St.   (Mercer/Broadway)   212-431-5521

This bright, colorful, and playful (not to mention reasonable), boutique carries many hard-to-find European designers. Whether you're looking for a sexy natural-colored leather skirt or multi-colored poncho, everything is delightful and bright. It also has fabulous accessories for those in the market for wardrobe overhauls. **Best Find: Beautiful People open knit wrap dress $300.**

· *Crêpe and lycra pants $165*

· **Alicia Lawhon** · **Aria** · **Beautiful People** · **Buquet** · **Chang**
· **Girlfriend** · **Icon** · **Imagine This** · **Liquid** · **LM Lulu** · **Lux**
· **Sue Wong** · **Sweet Romeo** · **Tark 1**

☺ M-Sun 11-8
Exchange w/in 5 days w/ receipt.

C | A- | A- | 3

Arizona
91 Spring St.   (Broadway/Mercer)   212-941-7022

Filled with a good selection of classic leather jackets, pants, and skirts, Arizona carries something for everyone at relatively reasonable prices. When you're shopping, remember that leather exaggerates body shapes and choose accordingly. **Best Find: Drawstring A-line leather skirt $324.**

· *Lambskin leather pants $379*

· **Zabari**

☺ M-Sun 11-8
Store credit w/in 30 days w/ receipt.

C+ | C | A- | 3

Mavi
510 Broome St. (W. Broadway/Thompson) 212-625-9458

You can never have too many jeans. You can never have too many jeans. You can never have too many jeans. At Mavi, all jeans are made for slender bodies. Shoppers who make the cut will find a large selection and prices that are seductively low.

· *Jeans $52*

· **Mavi**

☺ M-Sun 11-8
Refund w/ tags and receipt.

| B | | A- | | A- | | 🐷2 |

Catherine
468 Broome St.   (@ Greene)   212-925-6765

This colorful shop brightens up the neighborhood, with its typically dark boutiques. Catherine's vibrant, pretty dresses, v-shaped multi-colored skirts, and countless shawls and ponchos will brighten your mood, too. The cuts are fitted and delicate, but surprisingly sturdy. So if you're taken aback by the slightly steep prices, remember that these clothes are a long-term investment. **Best Find: Heavy-weave multicolored wool v-bottom skirt $312**.

· *Cashmere sweater $180*

· **Catherine**

☺ M-Sat 11-7, Sun 12-7
Store credit w/ receipt.

| B+ | | A- | | A- | | 🐷3 |

Debra Moorefield
466 Broome St.   (Mercer/Greene)   212-226-2647

The pickings are slim at Debra Moorefield, but the styles are clean and classic. The fine quality of the button-down shirts, slacks, and wrap coats are a treat for your wardrobe, but by no means essential.

· *Camel-hair coat $700*

· **Deborah Moorefield · P-10**

☺ M-Sat 12-7, Sun 12-6
Return w/in 7 days w/ receipt and tags.

| B+ | | B- | | A- | | 🐷3 |

Kate Spade
454 Broome St.   (@ Mercer)   212-274-1991

Don't walk into Kate Spade's boutique expecting a cutesy emporium full of girly handbags. The space is sleek and modern and devoid of any decorations but the bags themselves, which offer plenty to look at: they come in every size, color and fabric, an array sufficient for any destination or time of day. Also, check out the man-tailored pajamas and Macintosh raincoats. **Best Find: Leather shoulder clutch $465**.

· *Wool shoulder bag $350*

· **Kate Spade**

☺ M-Sat 11-7, Sun 12-6
Store credit w/in 14 days.

| C+ | | A- | | A- | | 🐷3 |

Calypso on Broome
424 Broome St. (Crosby/Lafayette) 212-274-0449

This Broome Street location has the same colorful spirit as its sister stores, with an emphasis on formal wear. Add some spice to an otherwise drab wardrobe from the shop's endless supply of bright, original pieces. The bags, scarves, shawls, and other items will leave you swooning.

· *Malatesta embroidered shawl $200*

· 3 Dots · Anna K · Beautiful People · Brooklyn Handknits
· Calypso · Coup de Pied · Diab'less · Dosa · Lluis
· Malatesta · Matilde · Miguelena · Paul & Joe

🕑 M-Sat 11-7, Sun 11-6
Store credit w/in 10 days w/ receipt.

A- | A+ | A- |

Alpana Bawa
41 Grand St. (W. Broadway/Thompson) 212-965-0559

The Indian-inspired designs at Alpana Bawa are not for the faint of heart. The bright colors and unusual cuts make for striking ensembles which are best suited for occasions when being noticed is the goal. **Best Find: Turquoise cashmere coat with quilted hood $1600.**

· *Silk beaded top $450*

· **Alpana Bawa**

🕑 M-F 11-7, Sat 12-7, Sun 12-6
Store credit w/in 14 days w/ receipt.

B+ | A- | A- |

Yaso
62 Grand St. (Wooster/W. Broadway) 212-941-8506

This huge store can accommodate virtually everyone and her mother and its eclectic collection makes it the perfect place for them to stay together. Whether you're the twentysomething looking for a cool outfit to wear on the town or the mom paying for the outfit while trawling for a sophisticated shawl of your own, Yaso will satisfy your desires. **Best Find: Pink velvet cap-sleeve romantic skirt $175.**

· *Rayon open-back dress $199*

· **Conchi · Cow Girls · Dutchess · Inshalla · Irkasweater**
· **Lotta · Luna · Michael Stars · Post · Stuff · The Wonder Tees**

🕑 M-Sun 11-7
Store credit w/in 7 days.

B | B+ | A- |

IF
94 Grand St. (Greene/Mercer) 212-334-4964

If you are bored to death by either ultraconservative styles or flat-out frumpy frocks, this boutique may be the upper your wardrobe needs. The store features upscale cutting-edge designs—both American and European—and carries wearable everyday clothes that won't put you to sleep.

· *Commes des Garçons white cotton shirt $245*

· **Comme des Garçons · Ivan Grindahl · Johnny Farah · Linea S**
· **Martin Margiela · NY Industrie · Veronique Branquinho**

🕑 M-Sat 11-7, Sun 11-6:30
Store credit w/in 7 days w/ receipt.

C+ | A- | A |

Yohji Yamamoto
103 Grand St.   (@ Mercer)   212-966-9066

At first glance this clothing may seem a bit bizarre, but a closer inspection reveals its brilliant design. The cuts are often severe and the fabric is often black. If you're looking for an outfit that will make you feel sleek, sharp, and powerful, Yohji will probably come through. His extraordinary garments are surprisingly wearable and will give an enduring boost to any wardrobe.

· *Wool sweater $445*

· **Yohji Yamamoto**

☺ M-Sat 11-7, Sun 12-6
Store credit w/in 5 days w/ receipt.

| C+ | A | A+ | |

E. Vogel Boots & Shoes
19 Howard St.   (Broadway/Lafayette)   212-925-2460

Forget Mr. Pink. True Masters of the Universe go beyond the made-to-measure shirt, into the realm of the bespoke (custom-made) shoe. If you're ready to take this step, go to E. Vogel and get yourself a pair of their traditional English riding boots, the only style available for women. The boots can be made in three types of leather: domestic, French calf, and French baby calf. Prices begin at $635 and go as high as $1200.

· *English riding boots $635-$1200*

· **E. Vogel**

☺ M-F 8-4:30, Sat 8-2
All sales final.

| B+ | C+ | A | |

Nolita &
Little Italy

10013 New York	Label
A Détacher	Language
Amy Chan	Lucien Pellat-Finet
Blue Bag	Malia Mills Swimwear
Calypso St. Barth*	Mark Schwartz
Center for the Dull	Mary Jaeger
Christopher Totman	Mayle
Claire Blaydon	Montgomery
Demoo Parkchoon Moo	Nylon Squid
Dö Kham	P.A.K.
Dressing Room	Pearl River*
Elma Blint et al	Plum
Fifty	Red Wong
Fuchsia	Resurrection*
Hedra Prue	Sample
Henry Lehr	Seize sur Vingt
Henry Lehr (T-shirt store)	Sigerson Morrison
Hunco Trading	Steinberg & Sons
INA*	Tracy Feith
Jade	Wang
Jamin Puech	X-Large
Janet Russo	Zero
Kinnu	

*Additional locations can be found
in the Multiple Store Index pp. 152-159.

LAFAYETTE STREET

X-Large
267 Lafayette St.   (Prince/Spring)   212-334-4480

Displaced LA girls take note: this shop should remind you of home. The skate-boarder style probably works better on the West Coast than here, but this boutique definitely has a following. Unfortunately, the selection for women is limited to a couple of shift dresses and baby T-shirts.

· *Mini sleeveless summer dress $150*
· **Mini by X-Large**

☺ M-Sun 12-7
Store credit w/in 30 days w/ receipt.

| B | B | B- | |

Label
265 Lafayette St.   (Prince/Spring)   212-966-7736

Twentysomething downtowners like the handmade look of these clothes. The house line is nothing out of the ordinary and certainly no bargain, but standards including slim-cut pants, A-line skirts, and wool racing-style jackets may add flair to your wardrobe.

· *Wool racing jacket $142*
· **Label**

☺ M-Sun 12-7
Exchange or store credit w/ receipt. No time period.

| B- | C+ | B- | |

Nylon Squid
222 Lafayette St.   (Spring/Broome)   212-334-6554

The ambience at Nylon Squid is reminiscent of the space station in 2001, and the clothes match the atmosphere. You'll find parachute skirts, nylon pants and jackets, and other fashion-forward items. Though the aesthetic might lean toward mid-century modernism, Nylon Squid is no Target commercial. The cloven-toed booties which greet you when you walk in the door are ample proof of that. This store is for well-heeled downtowners who like their clothes chic, urban, and futuristic, and who aren't averse to a tinge of goth perversity.

· *Gray cotton balloon-bottom skirt $199*
· **Born Free · Donna de Francq · Free Tibet · Urban Action · Vexed Action · YMC**

☺ M-Sun 12-7
Store credit w/in 7 days.

| C+ | B+ | B | |

Center for the Dull
216 Lafayette St.   (Spring/Broome)   212-925-9699

Time stands still in this psychedelic space, where racks of retro-clothes from Wrangler jeans to Candies shoes (with original tags) rest against toxic-smelling walls of pink cotton candy-like sound insulation. Brave the potential biohazard for a good laugh.

· *Vintage Lee jeans $35*
· **N/A**

☺ M-Sun 12-7
All sales final.

| C | A- | C+ | |

service | presentation | quality | expense

NOLITA AND LITTLE ITALY

Jade
280 Mulberry St.   (Houston/Prince)   212-925-6544

Jade carries fewer pieces than its sister store Calypso and focuses on ethnic, feminine dress-wear. It is an excellent source for delicate beaded, sequined, and embroidered tops, and it carries ethnically-influenced bags.

· *Jade beaded chiffon shell $75*

· **3 Dots · Amy Friday · Antik Batik · Bindia · Calypso · Diab'less · Dosa · Hector Knits · Jade · Laura Vogel · Malatesta · Miguelena · Monah Li · Noir Ebene · Petit Bateau · Plenty**

☺ M-Sat 11-7, Sun 12-6
Store credit w/in 10 days w/ receipt.

B	A-	A-	

Amy Chan
247 Mulberry St.   (Prince/Spring)   212-966-3417

The trademark tile bags are arranged by color and size in piles throughout the store, making browsing easy and enjoyable. These bags are excellent for women who want a nighttime bag with an edge.

· *Medium-size silk sari bag with plastic tile mosaic $280*

· **Amy Chan · Maria Wagner · Thé de la Menthe**

☺ M-Sat 12-7, Sun 12-5
Store credit w/in 14 days.

C+	A-	A-	

Language
238 Mulberry St.   (Prince/Spring)   212-431-5566

Language speaks to women at the forefront of downtown fashion. The store carries everything from eccentric wool ponchos and ruffled chokers to vintage evening wear and Earl jeans. It caters to hip skinny women, carries lesser-known European designers, and is always one step ahead of the pack.

· *Jules leather pants $475*

· **Azzedine Alaïa · Bajra · Bella Freud · Brian Wolks Ruffian · Cashmere Studio · Chlöe · Culture · Daya Richter · Earl Jeans · Fred Sathal Paris · James Perse · Jemima Khan · Jerome L'huiller · Johanna Ho · John Bartlett · Jules · Language Vintage · Lisa Johnson · M. Ellen Bags · Minthe & Simonsen · Phillip Tracey · Rosa Cha · Sibella Pavenstedt · Tufi Duek · Urvashi**

☺ M-Sat 11-7, Th 12-8, Sun 12-6
Store credit w/in 14 days w/ receipt.

A	A-	A-	

Tracy Feith
209 Mulberry St.   (Spring/Kenmare)   212-334-3097

Tracy Feith's boutique is irresistible: the store is beautifully designed, and the clothes, with their bright colors and beautiful patterns, are sure eye-candy. The pieces are for the thin, the young, and the bold, though anyone can respond to the accessories, particularly the phenomenal handbag selection.

· *Fleece eyelet cardigan $188*

· **Tracy Feith**

☺ M-Sat 11-7,Sun 12-7
Store credit w/in 10 days w/ receipt.

A	A+	A	

MULBERRY STREET

Malia Mills Swimwear
199 Mulberry St.   (Spring/Kenmare)   212-625-2311

Malia Mills is a compact swimwear boutique that recognizes that Mother Nature mixes and matches upper and lower bodies and a swimsuit store should do the same. You can also pick up cute scarf-tops and sarong-style skirts for aprés-swim.

· *Viscose/spandex bikini $160*

· **Andrea Stuart · Costo · Malia Mills · Sunblock**

☺ M-Sun 12-7
Store credit w/in 14 days.

A- | B | A- | 🐷 3

Red Wong
181 Mulberry St.   (Kenmare/Broome)   212-625-1638

The store's dark, too-modest facade gives no hint of the treasures within. You won't find anything here that's conventional, either in style or cut, but you will find many up-and-coming designers who are worth discovering. **Best Find: Jacquard reversible bustle skirt $185.**

· *Felt skirt with mirrored panel $185*

· **Anais · Carla Dawn Behrle · Christina Davis · Juliet Horn · Liz Collins · Mike Paré · Olivia Eaton · Red Wong**

☺ M-Sat 12-8, Sun 12-6
Store credit w/in 90 days w/ receipt.

A | B | B | 🐷 3

Hedra Prue
281 Mott St.   (Houston/Prince)   212-343-9205

This store is a meeting place where you'll find both well-known and lesser-known designer labels in items such as velvet suits, denim trench coats, and A-line skirts. However, the store is quite small and carries only a few pieces from each line. Browse frequently to see which new designers are in stock. **Best Find: Fitted velvet suit by Martin, jacket $385, pants $220.**

· *Denim coat lined with hot pink flannel $355*

· **Autumn Cashmere · Denise Williamson · Juicy Couture · Ulla Johnson · Rebecca Dannenberg · Wayne Cooper**

☺ M- Sat 11:30-7:30, Sun 12-6:30
Exchange w/in 7 days w/ tags and receipt.

C+ | B | A- | 🐷 3

Calypso St. Barth
280 Mott St.   (Houston/Prince)   212-965-0990

Think pink! Also blue, and green, yellow, red, orange and purple. Black is banned at this trend-setting Caribbean boutique, where goods are arranged according to the colors of the rainbow. Add some spice to an otherwise drab wardrobe from an endless supply of bright, original pieces. The bags, scarves and other items will leave you swooning. **Best Find: Small cow-print multi-colored bag $350.**

· *Cordoroy petticoat skirt $140*

· **3 Dots · Anna K · Beautiful People · Brooklyn Handknits · Calypso · Coup de Pied · Diab'less · Dosa · Lluis · Malatesta · Matilde · Miguelena · Paul & Joe**

☺ M-Sat 11-7, Sun 12-6
Store credit w/in 10 days w/ receipt.

C- | A- | A- | 🐷 3

Janet Russo
262 Mott St.   *(Houston/Prince)*   212-625-3297

Think Betsy Johnson without the craziness. This boutique offers romantic cocktail dresses, sweet sweater sets, and delicate bags in floral prints. But don't be fooled by their old-ladyish qualities—once you try them on, you'll see that these clothes aren't for grandma. **Best Find: Corduroy ruffle wrap dress $250.**

· *Knee-length evening dress with velvet straps
  and lace overlay $325*
· **Celine** · **Cristina Gavioli** · **Diab'less** · **Janet Russo**
· **Marybeth** · **Tova**

☺ M-Sat 11-7, Sun 12-6
Store credit w/in 5 days w/ receipt.

B		B+		B+	

A Détacher
262 Mott St.   *(Houston/Prince)*   212-625-3380

Featuring a very limited selection from up-and-coming designer Mona Kowalska, A Détacher's clothes are meant to look a little rough around the edges. Neutral-colored jackets and skirts play with necklines and cuts, allowing someone who prefers the classics to introduce a modern note to her wardrobe.

· *Camel-colored wool top $180*
· **Mona Kowalska**

☺ T-Sat 12-7, Sun 1-6
Store credit w/in 30 days w/ receipt.

A-		B-		B	

Demoo Parkchoon Moo
262 Mott St.   *(Houston/Prince)*   212-941-7117

Interpretative clothing should generally be approached carefully. So be forewarned when you check out the clothing in this underground Korean boutique. Most is either shapeless or constructed so oddly that the wearer looks more like a work of art than a stylish human. But someone with a good eye may be able to find a provocative and unique addition to her wardrobe.

· *Red wool turtleneck sweater with x-long sleeves $230*
· **Demoo Parkchoon Moo**

☺ M-Sun 12-7
Refund w/in 3 days.

C-		A		A-	

Christopher Totman
262 Mott St.   *(Houston/Prince)*   212-925-7495

Christopher Totman's boutique is not marked by trends or seasons, yet it manages to remain current. The sleek basics include micro-corduroy slim pants and matching puffy vests in the winter and bias-cut textile skirts for summer. **Best Find: Puffy micro-corduroy vest $230.**

· *Raw silk shirt $250*
· **Christopher Totman**

☺ M-Sat 11-7, Sun 12-6
Exchange w/in 3 days w/ receipt.

A-		A-		A-	

MOTT STREET

Jamin Puech
252 Mott St.   *(Houston/Prince)*   *212-334-9730*

There is no contemporary designer who makes bags more beautiful than Jamin Puech. Intricately beaded, sequined, and embroidered, they are more like artwork than accessories, and you may have trouble leaving the store without carrying one off. You'll also find stunning velvet scarves with superlative beading that are ideal to dress up a simple wool coat.

· *Sequined bag with velvet interior $350*

· **Jamin Puech**

☺ M-Sat 11-7, Sun 12-6
Store credit w/in 10 days.

| **B** | **B+** | **A+** | |

Sigerson Morrison
242 Mott St.   *(Houston/Prince)*   *212-219-3893*

Sigerson Morrison has combined classic styles with modern color usage and subtly innovative shapes to create some of the most sensational-if-hard-to-wear shoes in the city. Try an orange mule or a green square-toed pump, or go with the beautifully-updated black leather boot. **Best Find: Orange velvet flat $210**.

· *Sabrina heel with small buckle $275*

· **Louison** · **Penn & Alex** · **Tambu** · **Sigerson Morrison**

☺ M-Sat 11-7, Sun 12-6
Store credit w/in 7 days.

| **C+** | **B-** | **A-** | |

P.A.K.
229 Mott St.   *(Prince/Spring)*   *212-226-5167*

This store took notice of the fact that somewhere along the way basics got a bit boring, and it decided to do something about it. The results are familiar items, like trousers and fleece motor-cross jackets, updated to conform to current styles with a bit more flair than usual.

· *White cotton oxford $145*

· **P.A.K**

☺ M-Sat 12:30-7:30, Sun 1-6
Store credit w/in 7 days w/ receipt.

| **B+** | **B+** | **A-** | |

Zero
225 Mott St.   *(Prince/Spring)*   *212-925-3849*

As is typical of area boutiques, Zero has a minimalist approach to both store decor and clothing design. Its selection of casual wear is sleek, modern and mainly black—just the thing for the slim, chic downtowner. Its Bloom bags are the perfect accessory for any outfit.

· *Denim tab pant $199*

· **Bloom** · **Lizzy Disney**

☺ M-F 12:30-7:30, Sat-Sun 12:30-6:30
Store credit w/in 7 days.

| **B** | **B** | **A-** | |

Wang
219 Mott St. *(Prince/Spring)* **212-941-6134**

A small store can still feature a great selection, if the owner has style and smarts. Wang's owner must qualify, because the clothes here, though not for everyone, are definitely worth checking out. They're unique and refreshing to a shopper who's had her fill of cookie-cutter clothes. **Best Find: Corduroy skirt with pleat $130.**

· *Nylon stretch pants $170*

· **Cheung Fat** · **Wang**

☉ M-Sun 12-7
Exchange w/in 7 days w/ receipt.

C+	B	A-	

Resurrection
217 Mott St. *(Prince/Spring)* **212-625-1374**

Resurrection is the shop where grandma's clothes come back to life. The hand-me-downs are arranged in an orderly fashion, and the racks are often filled with pieces that you might find in the editorial layouts of this month's fashion magazines. This season, for example, there is an ample supply of crocheted shawls and jeans skirts. Because of the excellent condition and the unusually high style, the clothes here are a bit pricier than at other vintage stores.

· *Pucci cotton shirt $225*

· **N/A**

☉ M-Sat 12-8, Sun 12-7
All sales final.

C	B+	B-	

Claire Blaydon
202A Mott St. *(Spring/Kenmare)* **212-219-1490**

This itsy-bitsy boutique has a teensy-weensie selection. Blaydon focuses on knitwear throughout the year, and this winter it features fur-trimmed sweaters, dresses, skirts, and Fendi-esque bags. Not a spot for wardrobe stockpiling, but a good place to get a reasonably-priced piece that few others will be wearing. **Best Find: Pink mohair/rabbit-trimmed bag with leather strap $210.**

· *Summer dress $150*

· **Claire Blaydon** · **Marimekko**

☉ M-Sat 11-7, Sun 11-6
Store credit or exchange w/in 3 days w/ receipt.

C	C+	B-	

Henry Lehr (T-shirt store)
268 Elizabeth St. *(Houston/Prince)* **212-343-0567**

Obsessive-compulsive T-shirt lovers will adore Henry Lehr, where the merchandise is arranged by name brand and then color. You'll never go back to Hanes after you get a load of this large selection of wonderfully wearable shirts.

· *3 Dots long-sleeve tee with collar $49*

· **3 Dots** · **Drawers** · **Fake** · **G** · **Gretel's Clogs** · **Hard Tail** · **JET** · **Juicy Couture** · **Michael Stars**

☉ M-Sun 11-7
Store credit w/ receipt & tags.

A-	A-	A-	

ELIZABETH STREET

Sample
268 Elizabeth St. (Houston/Prince) 212-431-7866

This petite, immaculate boutique carries knitwear in many appealing colors. The silk/cotton blend fabric is crafted into sensuous cuts that are the perfect choice for mature working women. Couple the sweaters with a pair of slim-cut pants. Sample also carries a selection of fine towels and bath products.

· *3/4 sleeve rayon sweater $165*

· **Sample**

☺ T-Sat 12-7, Sun 12-5
Store credit w/in 7 days w/ receipt.

A-		B		A-	

Blue Bag
266 Elizabeth St. (Houston/Prince) 212-966-8566

Blue Bag carries unique bags from all over the world for every occasion. Whether it's a small and beaded evening number or just another leather shoulder bag that you're after, you'll find it here. **Best Find: Sequoia natural leather bag $175.**

· *Hervé Chepalier medium bag $95*

· **Antik Batik** · **Blue Bag** · **Bronti Bay** · **Delphine Pariente**
· **Facteur Celeste** · **Hervé Chepalier** · **Hoa Hoa** · **Idea Plus**
· **Johanna Braitbart** · **Kristina Richards** · **Marie Bouvero**
· **Marion Godart** · **Minima Moralia** · **Rosamunda**
· **Samia Kamar**

☺ M-Sun 11-7
Store credit w/in 14 days.

A-		B		A-	

Mayle
252 Elizabeth St. (Houston/Prince) 212-625-0406

Fashion mavens flock to this unusual boutique that offers authentic downtown chic with a carefully chosen collection of new pieces designed by the owner as well as a few vintage ones. The merchandise is always a bit unusual (example: zebra- and leopard-print chiffon dresses) and the inventory is limited. **Best Find: Large leopard clutch $200.**

· *Zebra sheer chiffon dress $255*

· **Mayle**

☺ T-Sat 12-7, 12-6
Store credit w/in 7 days w/ receipt.

C		B-		B	

Elma Blint Et. Al.
245 Elizabeth St. (Houston/Prince) 212-965-0494

This store has come up with a novel way to battle customer boredom. It regularly features a different designer's line for a brief period of time, so just when you're likely to find the merchandise ho-hum, you'll find that it's been overhauled. The house line is the one constant, and the unifying theme is old styles with new twists.

· *Boucle long wool coat $550*

· **E-play** · **Elma Blint**

☺ T-Sat 12-7, Sun 12-6
Store credit w/in 7 days or 14 days for gifts.

A-		B		B+	

Seize sur Vingt
243 Elizabeth St.   (Houston/Prince)   212-343-0476

This former men's-only shirt boutique has recently introduced women's clothing. Beautiful tailor-made shirts of high-quality cottons, silks, and linens are both classic and stylish and suitable for work and casual wear. The selection is small, but any one of the exquisite pieces is sure to become a wardrobe staple. **Best Find: Thick cashmere twin-set with fur trim $640.**

· *Summer linen shirt $170*

· **Seize sur Vingt**

☺ M-Sun 12-7
Store credit w/in 14 days. Flexible w/gifts.

  A | A- | A |

Henry Lehr
232 Elizabeth St.   (Houston/Prince)   212-274-9921

Choosing is oh-so-difficult at Henry Lehr, where you'll want to take home everything you see. The best pieces from the most popular lines make it a sure winner for a younger clientele. **Best Find: Rebecca Taylor acrylic leopard hooded jacket $440.**

· *Ashley corduroys $170*

· **Ashley · Buzz 18 · Claudette · Earl Jeans · Helmut Lang · Henry Lehr · Icon · JET · Katayone Adeli · Nell · Rebecca Taylor**

☺ M-Sun 11-7
Store credit w/in 7 days.

  B | B+ | A- |

Steinberg & Sons
229 Elizabeth St.   (Houston/Prince)   212-625-1004

This eclectic boutique is quite small and carries only a few pieces from each line it stocks. Though there's not much to choose from, young people with a downtown sensibility may find a classic wrap dress or tattered tank-top in the style of Courtney Love that is to their liking.

· *Hunger World T-shirt $125*

· **Bait & Tackle · Built by Wendy · Diane Von Furstenberg · Hungerworld · Olga Kapustina · Richard Ruiz · Rookie · Valentine · Jean Yu**

☺ M-Sun 12-7
Exchange w/in 7 days w/ receipt.

  C+ | B- | B |

Lucien Pellat-Finet
226 Elizabeth St.   (Houston/Prince)   212-343-7033

Lucien Pellat-Finet is the hipster's N. Peal. The sweater boutique is nothing to write home about, but the cashmeres in modern cuts and patterns are exquisite and priced accordingly. Be prepared to spend a lot of money—a lot of money.

· *Orange cashmere zip cardigan $1450*

· **Lucien Pellat-Finet**

☺ M-Sat 11-6
Store credit w/in 7 days w/ receipt. Sale items final.

  C+ | B+ | A+ |

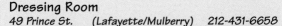

PRINCE STREET

Dö Kham
51 Prince St.   (Lafayette/Mulberry)   212-966-2404

The best Tibetan shop in Manhattan is a scarf/shawl haven filled with exquisite Pashminas in a gorgeous array of primary and pastel colors as well as mohair boas, silk-dyed shawls, and stunning floor-length wrap-skirts. It also carries matching raw silk bags, Tibetan-style cotton shirts, and exquisite bed covers, pillowcases and wall hangings. **Best Find: Silk wrap skirt $135.**

· *Pashmina shawl $275*

· **N/A**

☺ M-Sun 10-8
Store credit w/in 14 days.

| B+ | B+ | A- |

Dressing Room
49 Prince St.   (Lafayette/Mulberry)   212-431-6658

Crammed into a space no bigger than its name suggests, this tiny boutique features a variety of pieces by emerging designers. The clothes occasionally look as if they've been made by your friend with a sewing machine. If you find that sort of naive quality charming, Dressing Room will suit you especially well.

· *Dressing Room fleece poncho $78*

· **Albert Chan · Bionic Threads · Dressing Room Label · Grayson Riley · Minimum · Troy Smith**

☺ M-Sat 1-7, Sun 1-6
Store credit w/in 5 days.

| C+ | C+ | B- |

INA
21 Prince St.   (Mott/Elizabeth)   212-334-9048

Hand-me-downs have never been so chic. This designer resale shop houses an amazing selection of barely-worn clothing from the rich and stylish. For those who can't pay high-fashion prices the first time around, here's a second chance.

· *Paul Smith pants $65*

· **6 by Martin Margiela · A.P.C. · Alexander McQueen · Chaiken & Capone · Dolce & Gabbana · Fendi · Gucci · Helmut Lang · M Collection · Miu Miu · Prada · Susan Lazar · Tocca · Vivienne Westwood · Voyage**

☺ Sun-W 12-7, Th-Sat 12-8
All sales final.

| C+ | B- | A- |

Mary Jaeger
51 Spring St.   (Lafayette/Mulberry)   212-941-5877

Influenced by a sojourn in Asia, Mary Jaeger offers the mature woman a solid collection of Japanese-inspired clothing in fine silks, linens, and cashmere. There's a wonderful collection of gift items including scent-filled silk "dream pillows" to place over one's eyes and photo "memory albums" in quilted silk. **Best Find: Pleated cashmere scarf $225.**

· *Reversible shawls $440*

· **Mary Jaeger**

☺ T-F 1-7, Sat 12-7, Sun 12-5
Exchange w/in 7 days w/ receipt.

| A- | B | A |

service | presentation | quality | expense

N
O
L
I
T
A

A
N
D

L
I
T
T
L
E

I
T
A
L
Y

Fifty
50 Spring St., 2nd Fl. (Lafayette/Mulberry) 212-925-9833

The shopping experience at this store, which is hidden away on the second floor of its building, borders on claustrophobic. The owner's tiny selection of handmade designs barely fits into the even tinier space. If you can squeeze in, check out the small adorable evening bags and hand-made jewelry.

· *White cotton shirt with ruffle $140*
· **Casa Garcia · Lucy Barnes**
☺ T-Sun 12-7
Store credit w/in 7 days.

| B | C | B- | |

Mark Schwartz
45 Spring St.   (@ Mulberry)   212-343-9292

Upper East Side class meets downtown sophistication at Mark Schwartz's flagship store. The cozy shoe boutique features classic styles like pointy-toed pumps as well as current trends like snake-skin and pony hair. The one drawback is comfort. They might be great looking, but these shoes were not made for walking.

· *Black lace stiletto boots $595*
· **Mark Schwartz**
☺ T-Sun 12-7
Store credit w/in 30 days w/ receipt.

| B- | B+ | A- | |

Kinnu
43 Spring St.   (Mulberry/Mott)   212-334-4775

All the garments at Kinnu, primarily traditional Indian tops and pants, are made with imported fabric. The owner and his wife hand tie-dye much of the limited selection. An even bigger attraction than the clothes are the duvets and wall tapestries that may have you cooing.

· *Cotton peasant top $180*
· **Kinnu**
☺ M-Sun 11:30-7
Store credit w/in 10 days w/ receipt.

| B | B+ | B | |

Plum
85 Kenmare St.   (Cleveland/Mulberry)   212-431-7449

This hidden boutique brings Japanese ultra-chic to a wearable level—though just barely. The parachute skirts with adjustable hemlines and anti-flammable jackets verge on the bizarre. If you tend to be on the conservative side, the handmade clothes might not be for you; and the unconventional cuts are sometimes more chic than flattering. However, the prices are reasonable enough to allow you to be a little bit adventurous.

· *Nylon pants $70*
· **Plum**
☺ T-Sat 1-7, Sun 1-6
Store credit w/ tags & receipt.

| A- | B | B | |

BROOME STREET

Montgomery
396 Broome St.   *(Centre/Mulberry)*   212-941-8812

This off-the-beaten-path boutique may prove that quality and value are what truly determine success. Montgomery's textiles, painted fabric and unconventional cuts make for relatively inexpensive and striking evening wear. Favorites include painted stretch-velvet bias-cut gowns and asymmetric pony-hair skirts. **Best Find: Blue and black asymmetric pony-hair skirt $525.**

· *Floor-length "micro-batik" stretch-velvet gown $565*

· **Montgomery New York**

☺ T-Sat 1-8, Sun 2-8, M by appt. only
Store credit w/in 7 days.

A- | **B+** | **A** | 3

Pearl River
200 Grand St.   *(Mulberry/Mott)*   212-966-1010

This is a scaled-down version of Pearl River's Canal Street location. Style mavens have been coming here for years to stock up on everything from mandarin dresses and brightly-colored thermoses to beaded curtains and sandalwood soap.

· *Dresses $50*

· **N/A**

☺ M-Sun 10-7:30
Exchanges w/in 7 days.

C+ | **C+** | **B-** | 1

Hunco Trading
185 Centre St.   *(Hester/Canal)*   212-274-0122

Look past the tourist paraphernalia at this conventional Chinatown gift stand and don't give up too quickly in your quest for something special. Hanging among the clutter are a variety of very reasonably priced, sleeveless mandarin-style dresses.

· *Chinese print dress $45*

· **N/A**

☺ M-Sun 9-7
All sales final.

D+ | **C+** | **C+** | 1

Fuchsia
126 Baxter St.   *(Hester/Canal)*   917-990-9895 *(pgr)*

The mix of merchandise at this funky pink-shag-carpeted store is 80% factory samples, 20% vintage. Couture dresses and tacky period blouses hang side by side. And mark your calendar for the August and February sales, an absolute don't-miss.

· *Plein Sud cotton lycra suit $100*

Labels include: Agnès B. · Azzedine Alaïa · Cynthia Rowley · D&G · Daryl K · Deborah Moorefield · Donna Karan · Fendi · French Connection · Jean Paul Gaultier · Jill Stuart · Joseph · Karl Lagerfield · Kasper · Kenzo · Mark Eisner · Michael Kors · Missoni · Nicole Miller · Parallel · Paul Smith · Plein Sud · Prada · Ralph Lauren Black Label · Romeo Gigli · Searle · St. John · Stephen Sprouse · Tahari · Vivienne Westwood

☺ M 12-5, T-Sun 12-8
All sales final.

B+ | **B-** | **B+** | 2

service | presentation | quality | expense

10013 New York
157B Hester St. (Elizabeth/Bowery) *212-965-0888*

This Chinatown store, geared to younger shoppers, carries Korean and Japanese designers who all seem to have gone pocket-happy this season, putting compartments everywhere, perhaps in response to the tsunami of new cell-phone users. 10013 NY can be a bit pricey for what it carries, so catch the wave here during the summer sales.

· *Chinese-style dress $59*

· **N/A**

☉ M-Sun 11-7:30
Exchange w/in 7 days.

| B | C+ | C+ | |

NOLITA AND LITTLE ITALY

Lower East Side

ORCHARD STREET

Fragile
189 Orchard St.   (Houston/Stanton)   212-982-5437

If you're looking for popular French designers but having trouble finding them in New York, Fragile is your answer. This low-maintenance store also serves up obscure New York designers for the young and the hip.

· *Plein Sud vest $260*

· **Antoine et Lili** · **Bill Tornade** · **Corrine Cobson** · **Dōusidz**
· **Epoch** · **Epure** · **Erotokritos** · **Love Tanjane** · **Nicole Yu**
· **Only Hearts** · **Plein Sud** · **Xuly-bet**

☺ M-Sun 12-8
Store credit w/in 7 days.

| B- | D+ | B+ | |

DDC Lab
180 Orchard St.   (Houston/Stanton)   212-375-1647

Featuring techno music, magazines, and a coffee bar, the store, like its clothing, strives for an image. Luckily for the owners, there must be enough starving artists in the neighborhood who can afford to pay $200 for raw, unfinished clothing.

· *Jean jacket $200*

· **Davies-Keiller** · **DDC Lab** · **Roberto Crivello** · **Savania**

☺ M-Sat 12-8, Sun 12-6
Store credit anytime.

| B | B | B- | |

Zao
175 Orchard St.   (Houston/Stanton)   212-505-0500

Is it an art gallery or is it a clothing store? At Zao, the mix of futuristic, sci-fi clothing and contemporary art blurs the line between what's meant to be worn, and what's simply meant to be looked at. You may not know quite what to make of the robotic dogs and the projected pool of sea monkeys . . . but then, you also may not know what to make of the seriously avant-garde clothing.

· *Zao hooded cashmere poncho $600*

· **Alloy** · **Baleri Italia** · **Edra** · **Evans and Wong** · **Fred Flare**
· **Marie Mauriel** · **Maurizo Galante** · **Sosse** · **Stylewise**
· **Yashica** · **Zao**

☺ Sun-W 12-9, Th-Sat 12-11
Store credit w/in 14 days w/ receipt.

| C | A- | B | |

Alik Singer
163 Orchard St.   (Stanton/Rivington)   212-473-5922

Wool coats are a dime a dozen, but custom styles are hard to come by. At Alik Singer's spare store, the coat racks are given center stage to display the various possibilities in striking solid colors, including trench-coat styles in deep reds and blues—all made from thick, heavy wool.

· *Wool coat $800*

· **Alik Singer**

☺ T-Sun 10-6
Exchange w/in 7 days.

| B | C+ | B | |

service | presentation | quality | expense

Giselle
143 Orchard St. (Rivington/Delancy) **212-673-1900**

It's as if a tornado ripped a mid-western department store straight out of Kansas and dropped it on the Lower East Side: Giselle's dated mirror-and-formica interior is either charmingly anti-cool, or creepy and unnerving, depending on your taste. In any case, the store does carry a number of well-known designers at a discount that shoppers may appreciate.

· *Iceberg jeans $166*

· **Anna Sui** · **Basler** · **Escada Sport** · **Gispa** · **Hauber** · **Iceberg**
· **Mondi** · **Studio Ferre** · **Valentino**

☺ M-Th 9-6, F 9-4, Sun 9-6
Exchange w/in 7 days.

| C- | C- | A- | |

Klein's of Monticello
105 Orchard St. (@ Delancey) **212-966-1453**

One would never expect to find labels like these in this neighborhood, but Klein's of Monticello has been a Lower East Side fixture for over 25 years. The store boasts the best-quality merchandise of all the bargain-district stores and is great for distinguished women who like Madison Avenue's clothes, but not its prices.

· *Malo crew-neck sweater $500*

· **Les Copains** · **Luciano Barbera** · **Malo** · **Pucinelli Cashmere**
· **René Lezard** · **Vestimenta**

☺ M-Fri 10-5, Sun 10-5:30
Store credit.

| A- | C+ | A | |

Ber-Sel Handbags
75 Orchard St. (Broome/Grand) **212-966-5517**

This old-school Lower East Side discount store is the perfect place for the mature woman seeking modish designer bags at substantially reduced prices. Honor the spirit of the generations of Lower East Side ladies who have shopped around here, and don't let the store's shoddy appearance stand between you and these bargains.

· *Fendi baguette knock-off $96*

· **Carla Mancini** · **Cerruti 1881** · **Desmo** · **Focus**
· **Francesco Biasia** · **Furla** · **Hobo** · **Longchamp**
· **Nicole Miller** · **Perlina** · **Rodo**

☺ Sun-F 10-6
Refund w/in 7 days w/ receipt.

| B | C+ | B+ | |

Marmelade
172 Ludlow St. (Houston/Stanton) **212-473-8070**

On the Lower East Side you may often feel that you are shopping in someone's living room. You probably are at Marmelade, where what you get often depends on when you go. Its super late weekend hours make it a great pit stop while out bar-hopping.

· *Marmelade halter-top from vintage scarf $48*

· **N/A**

☺ M-Sun 1-8, F-S 1-12am
Store credit w/in 10 days.

| B | C | C | 1 |

LUDLOW STEET

TG 170
170 Ludlow St.   (Houston/Stanton)   212-995-8660

A Ludlow Street pioneer, TG 170 has shepherded several unknown designers into the major leagues. Its commitment to showcasing lesser-knowns is evident in its hip, diverse selection. It still pays homage to those it discovered and balances out its inventory with the trendy establishment. **Best Find: Karen Walker neck warmer $178.**

· *Katayone Adeli cords $136*

· **Albert Chan** · **Autumn Cashmere** · **Daryl K**
· **Freitag** · **Karen Walker** · **Katayone Adeli** · **Kooba**
· **Laura Reilly** · **Lauren Moffatt** · **Liz Collins**
· **Patty Shelabarger** · **Paul & Joe** · **Petit Bateau**
· **Pixie Yates** · **Rebecca Dannenberg** · **Ripcosa**
· **Ruby Tuesday** · **Sally Penn** · **Saucy Lulu** · **Souchi**
· **Terri Gillis** · **TG 170** · **The Wrights** · **Tooke**
· **Ulla Johnson** · **United Bamboo**

☺ M-Sun 12-8
Store credit w/in 7 days w/ receipt.

A | A- | A- |

Mary Adams
159 Ludlow St.   (Houston/Stanton)   212-473-0237

The custom-made Victorian-style gowns at Mary Adams would be suitable for a masquerade ball. Distinguished by iridescent silk taffeta with corsets and ballroom skirts, these designs can be a great alternative to conventional wedding gowns.

· *Stretch corset $172*

· **Dr. Boudoir** · **Mary Adams**

☺ Th-Sun 1-6 or by appt.
All sales final.

B+ | A- | A- |

Min Lee/105
105 Stanton St.   (@ Ludlow)   212-375-0304

Somewhat out of place in the self-consciously urban Lower East Side, Min Lee is the neighborhood's mainstream boutique. Its Siamese twin 105 is more at home in the area, but it seems silly that these two stores are separated under one roof. Customers can find long streamlined skirts and en vogue accessories in one room and animal print minis in the next. The extremely helpful sales people will be glad to show you around.

· *Uniform cotton and viscose pony-hair skirt $132*

· **Alice & Trixie** · **All Saints** · **Anni Kuan** · **Atsuro**
· **Beautiful People** · **Beverly Mehl** · **Coup de Pied**
· **Easel** · **Elizabeth Powell** · **Inca** · **Juicy Couture**
· **Lluis** · **Miah Y** · **Min Lee** · **Mitzi Baker** · **Nell** · **NY Industrie**
· **Only Hearts** · **People Used To Dream About the Future**
· **Sweet Romeo** · **Taehyun Kim** · **Tayama** · **Ted Baker**
· **TIMX** · **Un Aprés-Midi de Chien** · **Uni Form** · **XL**

☺ M-F 1-8, Sat-Sun 12-7
Store credit or exchange w/in 7 days.

A- | B+ | A- |

Patch 155
155 Rivington St. (Suffolk/Clinton) 212-533-9995

It's clear why this colorful, fun store is a neighborhood favorite for homemade urban clothes. The store's helpful owner/designer regularly features other small local designers. The clothes are often somewhat rough, and the prices rarely exceed $200.

· *Open knit poncho $200*

· **Annick · Cassandra · Flux · Hodge-Podge**
· **It's An Exciting Time To Be Me · Kaj Ani**
· **Maura McCarthy · Pick-a-Spot · Plum**

☺ W-Sun 12-8
Store credit w/in 10 days w/ tags.

| A- | B+ | B- | 2 |

Hello Sari
261 Broome St. (Allen/Orchard) 212-274-0791

A spectacular store, this misplaced hole-in-the-wall features an exquisite selection of hand-crafted scarves, saris and raw silk flats. The authentic Indian merchandise is beaded and embroidered on colorful silk chiffon and silk organza, making for great day or evening wear. Hello Sari's unbelievable prices make it the best bang for your buck in Manhattan. **Best Find: Raw silk shoes $30**.

· *Beaded sari $120*

· **N/A**

☺ Sat-Sun 12-7, call for weekly hours
All sales final.

| A | B | A- | 1 |

Tribeca & Chinatown

Behrle
China Silk & Handicrafts Corp.
Chinatown Souvenier Center
Mei Ling Gift Shop
New Age Designer
Oriental Gifts and Products
Pearl River*
Pow Fu Hao
St. Paula
Ting's Gift Shop
Tribeca Luggage
Wah Fun Company
Whole World Fashion Boutique

*Additional locations can be found
in the Multiple Store Index pp. 152-159.

service | presentation | quality | expense

GREENWICH STREET

Tribeca Luggage
295 Greenwich St. (Chambers/Warren) 212-732-6444

This store remembers that bags are a necessity, not just an accessory. It carries all the basic travel brands along with a first-rate selection of handbags and wallets. The house line of leather and pony-hair clutches is very current, and the wallets in multicolored leather, snake, and pony hair are truly fabulous. **Best Find: Pony-hair wallet $135.**

· *Purple snakeskin checkbook/wallet $150*

· **Briggs & Riley · Crypto · Dakota · Kipling · Le Bag**
· **Longchamp · Melo · Perlina · Timberland · Travel Well**
· **Vera Bradley · Walker · XS Baggage**

☺ M-F 10-7:30, Sat 11-6, Sun 12-5
Refund w/in 30 days w/ receipt.
Store credit afterwards.

B+ | B- | A- |

Chinatown Souvenier Center
60A Mott St. (Canal/Bayard) 212-344-9162

Ignore the name and the dozens of "I Love NY" T-shirts cluttering the front of this store and head directly for the rear, where you'll find some of the best silk dresses and jackets in all of Chinatown. The jackets come in three styles: cropped one-sided polyester, reversible silk hip-length, and down-filled short coats. A good haggler may stay within her budget and walk away with one of each.

· *Reversible pajama-style jackets $60*

· **N/A**

☺ M-Sun 10-9
Exchanges w/in 7 days.

C+ | C | C+ |

Pow Fu Hao
47 Mott St. (Bayard/Pell) 212-964-3858

This store has adapted Chinese styles to American dress. Find a cute selection of evening bags in Asian fabrics, and check out the skirts inspired by traditional Chinese gowns. The quality is not high, but neither are the prices.

· *Skirts $35*

· **N/A**

☺ M-Sun 10-8
All sales final.

C- | C- | C+ |

Wah Fun Company
43A Mott St. (Bayard/Pell) 212-227-1672

Although the proprietors of this narrow little store speak virtually no English, no problem: you won't need a translator to convey the information that you want everything in the place. The shop carries an extensive selection of silk clothing, including Chinese-style suits and dresses, but the accessories, including purses, fans, and little bags, are the must-haves.

· *Dresses $40*

· **N/A**

☺ M-Sun 10-7
All sales final.

C- | B- | B |

New Age Designer
38 Mott St.   *(@ Pell)*   *212-349-0818*

Your source for authentic Chinese attire. The store doubles as a fabric and custom design shop, and all outfits are made to order. Select the dress design of your choice from a book of patterns or provide one of your own, then choose your fabric from the most impressive collection of imported Hong Kong silks in all of New York. In over forty colors and patterns, the stunning textiles make even more stunning dresses.

· *Custom dress $250*

· **N/A**

☺ M-Sun 10-7
Cash only. All sales final.

A- | B+ | A |

St. Paula
19 Mott St.   *(Mosco/Chatham Sq.)*   *212-566-3083*

St. Paula's house line, made in Italy, is incredibly young and trendy. This season, the store is featuring halter tops and zipper-covered cargo pants. Enjoy trying them on in the spacious dressing rooms—an amenity which is absent elsewhere in Chinatown.

· *Pants $80*

· **St. Paula · Tea**

☺ M-Sun 11-8
Exchange w/in 7 days.

C+ | C+ | B |

China Silk and Handicrafts Corp.
18 Mott St.   *(Mosco/Chatham Sq.)*   *212-385-9856*

This store has the best gifts in Chinatown—especially amazing jewelry and exquisite silk pillowcases. You can also find traditional Chinese robes in silk and polyester blends, along with other basics like silk dresses and pajamas.

· *Pillow cases $20*

· **N/A**

☺ M-Sun 2-9
All sales final.

C+ | B | B- |

Whole World Fashion Boutique
17A Mott St.   *(Mosco/Chatham Sq.)*   *212-267-4210*

This is the only store in Chinatown which requires that you be buzzed inside. Once there, you'll find a mix of conservative, work-appropriate suits and traditional Asian-style dresses. The Chinese-fabric blouses are worth checking out though, like much of the merchandise, seem a bit overpriced.

· *Shirts $50*

· **N/A**

☺ M-Sun 11-7
Exchange w/in 7 days.

D | C+ | C+ |

DOYERS STREET

Ting's Gift Shop
18 Doyers St.   *(Pell/Bowery)*   212-962-1081

Run by a mother and daughter, Ting's is the real deal in Chinatown. The store has a small selection of exceptional and authentic products. The mule-style slippers are particularly irresistible. Whether you're wearing them or gifting them, they'll make your friends wonder when you had the time to slip away to Hong Kong.

· *Beaded slippers $7*

· **N/A**

☺ M-Sun 11-9
Exchanges w/in 7 days.

C+	B	A-

Pearl River
277 Canal St.   *(@ Broadway)*   212-431-4770

The only department store in the neighborhood is a favorite of locals and day-trippers alike. Pearl River is packed to the gills with every imaginable type of merchandise, much of it amazingly cheap. Style mavens have been coming here for years to stock up on everything from mandarin dresses and brightly-colored thermoses to beaded curtains and sandalwood soap. If you haven't been here yet, a visit is a must.

· *Dresses $50*

· **N/A**

☺ M-Sun 10-7:30
Exchanges w/in 7 days.

C+	C+	B-

Mei Ling Gift Shop
213 Canal St.   *(Mulberry/Baxter)*   212-625-0657

Located on Chinatown's main street, this store is easily mistaken for a souvenir shop. But, like other, similar stores in the neighborhood, Mei Ling carries a variety of Chinese dresses (in addition to skyscraper snow globes). The selection is limited, but you can usually find a choice of colors in each size.

· *Knee-length flower print dress $50*

· **N/A**

☺ M-Sun 9:30-9:30
Exchange w/in 14 days w/ receipt.

C-	C-	C+

Oriental Gifts and Products
96 Bayard St.   *(Mulberry/Baxter)*   212-608-6670

Look through the limited selection for reasonably priced Chinese pajama suits in both short and long sleeves. The real steals are the slippers and shoes, including woven plastic mules and velour Mary Janes. At four or five dollars a pop, you can buy the whole collection.

· *PJ's $40*

· **N/A**

☺ M-Sun 10:30-8
Store credt w/in 14 days w/ receipt.

C	C	B-

service | presentation | quality | expense

Behrle
89 Franklin St. (Church/Broadway) 212-334-5522

Custom leather has never been so fashionable. The designer, Carla Dawn Behrle, makes sexy leather goods in bright, vibrant colors as well as the neutrals. Behrle focuses mainly on pants, which can be made in straight leg, bootleg or capri, to name a few. The styles are glamorous and Behrle's clothes are a favorite among celebrities. The designs are both custom and special order, depending on your needs.

· *Leather pants $1000*

· **Carla Dawn Behrle**

⊙ T-Sat 12-7
Store credit w/in 7 days. Custom items final.

B+ | C+ | A |

Lower Manhattan

Abercrombie & Fitch
Ann Taylor*
Barneys New York
Banana Republic*
Brooks Brothers*
Burlington Coat Factory*
Coach*
Country Road*
Century 21
Express*
Gap*
Georgiou
J. Crew*
Lafayette NY 148
Nine West*
Tahari
The Limited
Victoria's Secret*

*Additional locations can be found
in the Multiple Store Index pp. 152-159.

service | presentation | quality | expense

Barneys New York
225 Liberty St. (World Financial Center) 212-945-1600

This is the only place to find truly edgy clothing in the financial district. The store is more of a boutique than its parent department store but it has enough of a selection to warrant a visit. Wall Street women who are feeling a little adventurous can find accessories here to spice up their dark suits. **Best Find: Cashmere gloves with suede trim $185.**

· *Wool/angora camel-colored skirt $350*

Labels include: Angel Sanchez · Antik Batik
· Azzedine Alaïa · Barneys New York · Capucine Puerari
· Chlöe · Christopher Totman · Colette Dinnegan
· Elspeth Gibson · Helmut Lang · Hussein Chalayan
· Jill Stuart · Lauren Moffatt · Les Prairies de Paris
· Lucien Pellat-Finet · Marc Jacobs · Martin Margiela
· Matthew Williamson · Milk Fed · Miu Miu
· Paul Smith · Phillip Chi · Prada · Rebecca Dannenberg
· Thimister · Tufi Duek · Uni Form · Vera Wang
· William B · Wynn Wink · Yigal Azrouel
· Yohji Yamamoto · Jean Yu · Zero

🕐 M-F 10-7, Sat 11-5, Sun 12-5
Refund w/in 30 days. Sale items w/in 7 days.

| C+ | B+ | A+ | |

Brooks Brothers
1 Church St.   (@ Liberty St.)   212-267-2400

The women's line is a fairly recent addition to the company brand. It consists of well-cut, simple pieces suitable for work or for such weekend activities as meeting a future mother-in-law. The reasonably-priced selection includes staples like cashmere sweaters, twin-sets, straight skirts, pleated slacks, and anything else you might wish to accessorize with a string of pearls.

· *Traditional black cocktail dress with 3/4 sleeve and boat collar $158*

· Brooks Brothers

🕐 M-F 8:30-6:30, Th 8:30-7, Sat 10-5
Refund w/in 1 year.

| B | B | A- | |

Burlington Coat Factory
45 Park Place   (W. Broadway/Church)   212-571-2631

Burlington's slogan may be "More than great coats®" but the great coats are still the main attraction. While the decor leaves something to be desired and the organization of the merchandise isn't particularly intelligible, you'll find an unparalleled selection of discount outerwear, ranging from classic pea coats to fur-collared dress coats.

· *CK mid-length wool coat $250*

Labels include: ABS · Albert Nippon · Anne Klein · BCBG
· Bisou Bisou · Calvin Klein · Evan-Picone
· French Connection · Halston · Hervé Benard
· Infinity · John Weitz · Jones New York
· Kasper · Larry Levine · Liz Claiborne · Marvin Richards
· Oleg Cassini · Paloma Picasso · Perry Ellis · Tahari

🕐 M-F 8-7, Sat 10-6, Sun 11-5
Store credit w/in 14 days w/ receipt.

| C- | D+ | B+ | |

Century 21
22 Cortland St.   (Church/Broadway)   212-227-9092

Otherwise known as paradise for the obsessed shopper, Century 21 offers the best discount clothing in New York. The place is near-total chaos—in part simply because it's a mob scene. It's definitely worth braving, because the dress that you trip over may have a Prada label and a rock-bottom price tag. Avoid lunch hours and rush hours if possible, but if you can't, go anyway.

· *Prada silk and chiffon dress $399*

Labels include: August Silk · BCBG · Betsey Johnson
· **Bill Blass · Bisou Bisou · Bulldog · Calvin Klein**
· **CK Calvin Klein · Costume National · Cynthia Steffe**
· **Diesel Style Lab · DKNY · Dolce & Gabbana · Free People**
· **Gucci · Helmut Lang · Industria · Jean Paul Gaultier**
· **Joseph Abboud · Kenar · La Perla · Lafayette NY 148**
· **Laundry · Mark Eisen · Polo Sport · Prada**
· **Ralph Lauren · Stephen Sprouse · Theory**
· **Tommy Hilfiger · Versace · XOXO**

☺ M-F 7:45-8, Th 7:45-8:30, Sat 10-7:30, Sun 11-6
Refund w/in 30 days w/ receipt.

| D | | D | | A- | | |

Abercrombie & Fitch
199 Water St. (South Street Seaport) 212-809-9000

All-American style is embodied in both the decor and the clothing at Abercrombie & Fitch. The line is geared toward the young, offering fashions such as cargo pants, embroidered jeans, boyfriend sweaters, namesake T-shirts and tanks, and more. The prices are quite reasonable, which makes this a great place for either back-to-school or post-graduate shopping. **Best Find: Wool hooded sweater $90**.

· *Cargo pants $60*

· **Abercrombie & Fitch**

☺ M-Sat 10-9, Sun 11-8
Refund anytime w/ receipt.

| C+ | | B | | B | | |

Georgiou
225 Liberty St. (World Financial Center) 212-786-3497

Giorgiou was obviously created to serve the neighborhood's professionals, who need an ongoing supply of suits and other corporate attire. The store also carries evening dresses and sportswear in styles suitable for those who get their kicks from finance, not fashion.

· *Silk v-neck sweater $49*

· **Georgiou**

☺ M-F 10-7, Sat 11-5, Sun 12-5
Refund w/in 15 days.

| B | | C+ | | B- | | |

service | presentation | quality | expense

Lafayette NY 148
225 Liberty St. (World Financial Center) 212-571-5315

High-end style without the attitude. The garments in this store rival those in the best European fashion houses. The pieces are made of extraordinary fabrics with impeccable attention to detail. Designs are current, but not current enough to date too quickly. Lafayette NY 148 is an ideal destination for anyone desiring a luxurious wardrobe.

· *Wool coat with mink collar $798*

· **Lafayette NY 148**

☺ M-F 10-7, Sat 11-5, Sun 12-5
Refund w/in 7 days w/ receipt.
Store credit afterwards. Sale items final.

B | **B** | **A** |

Tahari
225 Liberty St. (World Financial Center) 212-945-2450

Tahari is a smart store that knows its customer well. The suit-based inventory is split between regular and petite sizes and emphasizes a day-to-evening style. The cocktail dresses double as suit pieces when paired with a matching jacket, and the delicate knit sweaters are also appropriate both during, and after, work. The separates can round out your weekend wardrobe, too.

· *Mohair/nylon mock turtle tank $198*

· **Tahari**

☺ M-F 10-7, Sat 11-5, Sun 12-5
Store credit w/in 10 days. Sale items final.

B+ | **B** | **A-** |

The Limited
World Trade Center Mall (West/Church) 212-488-9790

The more upscale parent company of Express, The Limited carries a less casual selection of inexpensive clothing. The fashions are very trendy and geared to the young, and can sometimes look downright cheap—so choose carefully.

· *Ballroom polyester skirt $99*

· **The Limited**

☺ M-F 8-8, Sat 11-6, Sun 12-5
Refund to method of payment.

C+ | **B+** | **B-** |

Indexes

MULTIPLE STORE INDEX
*This location featured in F.Y.I.

AGNÈS B.
1063 Madison Ave.*	(80th/81st)	212-925-4649
13 East 16th St.*	(5th/Union Sq. W.)	212-741-2585
116-118 Prince St.*	(Wooster/Greene)	212-925-4649

ANIK
1122 Madison Ave.*	(83rd/84th)	212-249-2417
1355 Third Ave.*	(77th/78th)	212-861-9840

ANN TAYLOR
2017 Broadway	(@ 69th)	212-873-7344
2380 Broadway	(@ 87th)	212-721-3130
645 Madison Ave.	(@ 60th)	212-832-9114
1055 Madison Ave.	(@ 80th)	212-988-8930
1320 Third Ave.	(@ 75th)	212-861-3392
850 Third Ave.*	(@ 52nd)	212-308-5333
1166 Sixth Ave.	(45th/46th)	212-642-4340
575 Fifth Ave.	(46th/47th)	212-922-3621
149 Fifth Ave.	(21st/22nd)	212-253-1445
225 Liberty St.	(World Financial Center)	212-945-1991

ANN TAYLOR LOFT
1492 Third Ave.	(84th/85th)	212-472-7281
150 East 42nd St.*	(@ Lexington)	212-885-8766

ANTHROPOLOGIE
85 Fifth Ave.*	(@ 16th)	212-627-5885
375 West Broadway*	(Spring/Broome)	212-343-7070

A/X ARMANI EXCHANGE
645 Fifth Ave.*	(@ 51st)	212-980-3037
568 Broadway*	(Houston/Prince)	212-431-6000

BANANA REPUBLIC
215 Columbus Ave.	(69th/70th)	212-873-9048
2360 Broadway	(@ 86th)	212-787-2064
1136 Madsion Ave.	(84th/85th)	212-570-2465
1131-1149 Third Ave.	(@ 67th)	212-288-4279
626 Fifth Ave.*	(@50th)	212-974-2350
130 East 59th St.	(@ Lexington)	212-751-5570
17 W. 34th St.	(5th/6th)	212-244-3060
107 East 42nd St.	(Grand Central Terminal)	212-490-3127
89 Fifth Ave.	(@ 16th)	212-366-4630
205 Bleeker St.	(6Th/MacDougal)	212-473-9570
550,552-554 Broadway	(@ Prince)	212-925-0308
South St. Seaport	(Pier 17)	212-393-1330
102 World Trade Center	(West/Church)	212-839-0952

BARAMI
1879 Broadway	(@ 62nd)	212-246-2930
1404 Second Ave.	(@ 73rd)	212-988-3470
485 Seventh Ave.	(@ 36th)	212-967-2990
136 Lexington Ave.	(@ 57th)	212-980-9333
375 Lexington Ave.	(41st/42nd)	212-682-2550

535 Fifth Avenue	(44th/45th)	212-949-1000
37 West 57th	(5th/6th)	212-308-0600
901 Sixth Ave.	(Manhattan Mall)	212-244-0370
119 Fifth Ave. *	(@ 19th)	212-529-2300

BARNEYS NEW YORK
| 660 Madison Ave. * | (60th/61st) | 212-826-8900 |
| 225 Liberty St. * | (World Financial Center) | 212-945-1600 |

BCBG MAX AZRIA
| 744 Madison Ave. * | (@ 66th) | 212-717-4225 |
| 770 Madison Ave. * | (64th/65th) | 212-794-7124 |

BEBE
1044 Madison Ave.	(79th/80th)	212-517-2323
1127 Third Ave. *	(@ 66th)	212-935-2444
805 Third Ave.	(@ 50th)	212-588-9060
1005 Fifth Ave.	(@ 15th)	212-675-2323

BETSEY JOHNSON
248 Columbus Ave. *	(71st/72nd)	212-362-3364
1060 Madison Ave.	(80th/81st)	212-734-1257
251 East 60th St.	(2nd/3rd)	212-319-7699
138 Wooster St.	(Houston/Prince)	212-995-5048

BIG DROP
| 1321 Third Ave. * | (75th/76th) | 212-988-3344 |
| 174 Spring St. * | (Thompson/W. B'way) | 212-966-4299 |

BROOKS BROTHERS
666 Fifth Ave. *	(52nd/53rd)	212-261-9440
385 Madison Ave. *	(@ 44th)	212-682-8800
1 Church St. *	(@ Liberty)	212-267-2400

BURLINGTON COAT FACTORY
| 707 West 23rd St. * | (@ 6th) | 212-229-1300 |
| 45 Park Place* | (Church/W. B'way) | 212-571-2630 |

CALYPSO
935 Madison Ave. *	(74th/75th)	212-535-4100
280 Mott St. *	(Houston/Prince)	212-965-0990
424 Broome St. *	(Crobsy/Lafayette)	212-274-0449

CHUCKIES
| 1073 Third Ave. * | (63rd/64th) | 212-593-9898 |
| 399 West Broadway* | (Spring/Broome) | 212-343-1717 |

CLUB MONACO
2376 Broadway	(@ 87th)	212-579-2587
1111 Third Ave. *	(@ 65th)	212-355-2949
160 Fifth Ave.	(@ 21st)	212-352-0936
520 Broadway	(@ Spring)	212-334-7444
121 Prince St.	(Wooster/Greene)	212-533-8930

COACH
| 2321 Broadway | (@ 84th) | 212-799-0041 |
| 710 Madison Ave. | (@ 63rd) | 212-319-1772 |

725 Fifth Ave., 3rd Fl.	(56th/57th)	212-355-2427
595 Madison Ave.*	(@ 57th)	212-754-0041
342 Madison Ave.	(@ 44th)	212-599-4777
South St. Seaport	(Pier 17)	212-425-4350
5 World Trade Center	(West/Church)	212-488-0080

COUNTRY ROAD

1130 Third Ave.	(@ 66th)	212-744-8633
335 Madison Ave.	(@ 43rd)	212-949-7380
156 Fifth Ave.	(20th/21st)	212-366-6999
411 West Broadway*	(Prince/Spring)	212-343-9544
South St. Seaport	(Pier 17)	212-248-0810

DAFFY'S

335 Madison Ave.	(@ 44th)	212-557-4422
135 East 57th St.	(Park/Lex)	212-376-4477
1311 Broadway*	(@ 34th)	212-736-4477
111 Fifth Ave.	(@ 18th)	212-529-4477
462 Broadway	(@ Grand)	212-334-7444

DARYL K

| 21 Bond St.* | (Lafayette/Bowery) | 212-777-0713 |
| 208 East 6th St.* | (2nd/3rd) | 212-475-1255 |

DETOUR

| 472 W. B'way* | (Houston/Prince) | 212-979-6315 |
| 154 Prince St.* | (Thompson/W. B'way) | 212-966-3635 |

DIANA & JEFFRIES

| 2062 Broadway* | (70th/71st) | 212-874-2884 |
| 1145 Madison Ave.* | (@ 85th) | 212-249-1891 |

EILEEN FISHER

341 Columbus Ave.	(76th/77th)	212-362-3000
521 Madison Ave.	(53rd/54th)	212-759-9888
1039 Madison Ave.	(79th/80th)	212-879-7799
103 Fifth Ave.	(17th/18th)	212-924-4777
314 East 9th St.	(1st/2nd)	212-529-5715
395 West Broadway*	(Spring/Broome)	212-431-4567

EMPORIO ARMANI

| 601 Madison Ave.* | (57th/58th) | 212-317-0800 |
| 110 Fifth Ave.* | (@ 16th) | 212-727-3240 |

EXPRESS

321 Columbus Ave.	(@ 75th)	212-580-5833
477 Madison Ave.	(@ 51st)	212-644-4453
722-728 Lexington Ave.	(@ 58th)	212-421-7246
733 Third Ave.	(@ 46th)	212-949-9784
901 Sixth Ave.	(@ 33rd)	212-971-3280
130 Fifth Ave.*	(@ 18th)	212-633-9414
7 West 34th St.	(5th/6th)	212-629-6838
South St. Seaport	(Pier 17)	212-693-0096
4 World Trade Center	(West/Church)	212-432-6074

FOGAL

| 680 Madison Ave.* | (61st/62nd) | 212-759-9782 |

| 510 Madison Ave.* | (@ 53rd) | 212-355-3254 |

FOPP'S
| 1265 Madison Ave.* | (90th/91st) | 212-831-3432 |
| 956 Lexington Ave.* | (69th/70th) | 212-794-8806 |

FORREAL BASICS
1200 Lexington Ave*	(81st/82nd)	212-717-0493
1335 Third Ave.	(76th/77th)	212-734-2105
1369 Third Ave.	(81st/82nd)	212-717-0493

FRENCH CONNECTION
304 Columbus Ave.	(74th/75th)	212-496-1470
1270 Sixth Ave.	(50th/51st)	212-262-6623
700 Broadway	(4th/Waverly)	212-473-4486
435 West Broadway*	(@ Prince)	212-219-1197

FURLA
| 727 Madison Ave.* | (63rd/64th) | 212-755-8986 |
| 430 West Broadway* | (Prince/Spring) | 212-755-8986 |

GAP
1988 Broadway	(@ 66th)	212-721-5304
2109 Broadway	(@ 73rd)	212-787-6698
2373 Broadway	(@ 86th)	212-873-1244
2551 Broadway	(95th/96th)	212-864-3600
335 Columbus Ave.	(@ 76th)	212-873-9270
1164 Madison Ave.	(@ 86th)	212-517-5763
734 Lexington Ave.	(@ 59th)	212-751-1543
1066 Lexington Ave.	(74th/75th)	212-879-9144
1131 Third Ave.	(@ 66th)	212-472-4555
1511 Third Ave.	(@ 85th)	212-794-5781
1466 Broadway	(@ 42nd)	212-768-2987
1212 Sixth Ave.	(@ 48th)	212-730-1087
680 Fifth Ave.	(@ 54th)	212-977-7023
527 Madison Ave.	(@ 54th)	212-688-1260
549 Third Ave.	(@ 36th)	212-213-6007
657 Third Ave.	(@ 42th)	212-697-3590
757 Third Ave.	(@ 47th)	212-223-5140
900 Third Ave.	(@ 54th)	212-754-2290
250 West 57th	(@ Broadway)	212-315-2250
60 West 34th St.	(@ Broadway)	212-643-8960
122 Fifth Ave.*	(@ 17th)	212-989-0550
113 East 23rd St.	(@ Park)	212-533-6670
133 Second Ave.	(@ St. Marks)	212-353-2090
1 Astor Pl.	(@ Broadway)	212-253-0145
South St Seaport	(Pier 17)	212-374-1051
World Trade Center	(West/Church)	212-432-7086

INA
| 101 Thompson St.* | (Prince/Spring) | 212-941-4757 |
| 21 Prince St.* | (Elizabeth/Mott) | 212-334-9048 |

INSTITUT
| 97 Spring St.* | (Mercer/B'way) | 212-431-5521 |
| 93 Spring St. | (Mercer/B'way) | 212-941-1970 |

INTERMIX
1003 Madison Ave.*	(77th/78th)	212-249-7858
125 Fifth Ave.*	(19th/20th)	212-533-9720

J. CREW
30 Rockerfeller Plaza	(5th/6th)	212-765-4412
91 Fifth Ave.	(16th/17th)	212-255-4848
99 Prince St.*	(@ Mercer)	212-966-2739
South St. Seaport	(Pier 17)	212-385-3500
230 World Trade Center Mall	(West/Church)	212-839-8378

JENNIFER TYLER
854 Madison Ave.*	(@ 70th)	212-772-8350
705 Lexington Ave.*	(@ 57th)	212-644-9175

JOAN & DAVID
816 Madison Ave.*	(68th/69th)	212-772-3970
104 Fifth Ave.*	(15th/16th)	212-627-1780

JOSEPH (PANT STORE)
804 Madison Ave.*	(67th/68th)	212-570-0077
115 Greene St.*	(Prince/Spring)	212-343-7071

JUNO
170 Fifth Ave.*	(@ 22nd)	212-647-9064)
550 Broadway*	(Prince/Spring)	212-925-6415

KENNETH COLE
353 Columbus Ave.	(76th/77th)	212-873-2061
107 East 42nd St.	(Park/Lexington)	212-949-8079
95 Fifth Ave.*	(@ 17th)	212-675-2550
597 Broadway	(Houston/Prince)	212-965-0283

LA GALLERIA LA RUE
12 West 23rd St.*	(5th/6th)	212-807-1708
385 Bleecker St.*	(@ Perry)	212-352-0961

LORD OF THE FLEAS
2142 Broadway*	(75th/76th)	212-875-8815
305 East 9th St.*	(1st/2nd)	212-260-9130
437 East 12th St.*	(1st/Ave A)	212-843-3269

LOUIS VUITTON
49 East 57th St.*	(Madison/57th)	212-371-6111
116 Greene St.*	(Prince/Spring)	212-274-9090

LUCA LUCA
1010 Madison Ave.*	(@78th)	212-288-9285
690 Madison Ave.*	(@ 62nd)	212-755-2444

MALO
814 Madison Ave*.	(@ 68th)	212-396-4721
125 Wooster St.*	(Prince/Spring)	212-941-7444

MANRICO
802 Madison Ave.	(67th/68th)	212-794-4200
140 Wooster St.	(Houston/Prince)	212-253-9877

MARAOLO

835 Madison Ave.	(69th/70th)	212-628-5080
782 Lexington Ave.*	(60th/61st)	212-832-8182
1321 Third Ave.	(75th/76th)	212-535-6225
551 Madison Ave.	(55th/56th)	212-308-8793

MIDALI

330 Columbus Ave.*	(75th/76th)	212-873-5451
1015 Madison Ave.*	(78th/79th)	212-879-2563

MIKAI

1425 Sixth Ave	(58th/CPS)	212-707-8770
397 Fifth Ave.	(35th/36th)	212-481-4941
647 Broadway*	(Bleeker/Bond)	212-529-8126
594 Broadway	(Houston/Prince)	212-431-3483

MONTMARTE

2212 Broadway*	(78th/79th)	212-875-8430
1754 Broadway	(56th/57th)	212-757-4252
247 Columbus Ave.	(71st/72nd)	212-721-7760

MORGANE LE FAY

746 Madison Ave.*	(64th/65th)	212-879-9700
67 Wooster St.*	(Spring/Broome)	212-219-7672

NEW YORK LOOK

2030 Broadway	(69th/70th)	212-362-8650
30 Lincoln Plaza	(62nd/B'way)	212-245-6511
570 Seventh Ave.	(@ 41st)	212-382-2760
551 Fifth Ave.	(@ 45th)	212-557-0909
468 West Broadway*	(Houston/Prince)	212-598-9988

NICOLE MILLER

780 Madison Ave.	(66th/67th)	212-288-9779
134 Prince St.*	(W. B'way/Wooster)	212-343-1362

NINE WEST

2305 Broadway	(@ 83rd)	212-799-7610
750 Lexington Ave.	(59th/60th)	212-486-8094
1195 Third Ave.	(69th/70th)	212-472-8750
184 East 86th St.	(Lex/3rd)	212-987-9004
1230 Sixth Ave.	(48th/49th)	212-397-0710
675 Fifth Ave.*	(53rd/54th)	212-319-6893
437 Fifth Ave.	(38th/39th)	212-725-0170
341 Madison Ave.	(@ 44th)	212-370-9107
757 Third Ave.	(47th/48th)	212-371-4597
115 Fifth Ave.	(@ 19th)	212-777-1752
577 Broadway	(Houston/Prince)	212-941-1597
South Street Seaport	(Pier 17)	212-791-2950
313 World Trade Center	(West/Church)	212-488-7665

OLD NAVY

150 W. 34th St.	(B'way/7th)	212-594-0049
610 Sixth Ave.	(@ 18th)	212-645-0663
503 Broadway*	(Spring/Broome)	212-226-0838

OLIVE & BETTE'S
1070 Madison Ave.*	(80th/81st)	212-717-9655
252 Columbus Ave.*	(71st/72nd)	212-579-2178

OTTO TOOTSI PLOHOUND
38 East 57th St.*	(Madison/Park)	212-231-3199
137 Fifth Ave.*	(20th/21st)	212-460-8650
413 West Broadway*	(Prince/Spring)	212-925-8931

PATAGONIA
426 Columbus Ave.*	(80th/81st)	917-441-0011
101 Wooster St.*	(Prince/Spring)	212-343-1776

PEARL RIVER
227 Canal St.*	(@ Broadway)	212-431-4770
200 Grand St.*	(Mulberry/Mott)	212-966-1010

POLO SPORT
888 Madison Ave.*	(@ 72nd)	212-434-8000
381 West Broadway*	(Spring/Broome)	212-625-1660

PRADA
841 Madison Ave.*	(@ 70th)	212-327-4200
724 Fifth Ave.*	(56th/57th)	212-664-0010

PRECISION
1310 Third Ave.*	(@ 75th)	212-879-4272
522 Third Ave.*	(@ 35th)	212-683-8812

PURDY GIRL
220 Thompson St.*	(Bleeker/3rd)	212-529-8385
540 LaGuardia Pl.*	(Bleeker/3rd)	646-654-6751

RESURRECTION
123 East 7th St.*	(1st/Ave. A)	212-228-0063
217 Mott St.*	(Prince/Spring)	212-625-1374

SACCO
2355 Broadway	(85th/86th)	212-874-8362
324 Columbus Ave.	(75th/76th)	212-799-5229
94 Seventh Ave.	(15th/16th)	212-675-5180
111 Thompson St.*	(Prince/Spring)	212-925-8010

SCOOP
1277 Third Ave.*	(73rd/74th)	212-744-3380
532 Broadway*	(Prince/Spring)	212-925-2886

SEARLE
1124 Madison Ave.	(83rd/84th)	212-988-7318
1035 Madison Ave.	(@ 79th)	212-717-4022
860 Madison Ave.	(70th/71st))	212-772-2225
609 Madison Ave.*	(57th/58th)	212-753-9021
1051 Third Ave.	(@ 62nd)	212-838-5990

THE ORIGINAL LEATHER STORE

256 Columbus Ave.	(71st/72nd)	212-595-7051
1100 Madison Ave.	(82nd/83rd)	212-585-4200
84 Seventh Ave.	(15th/16th)	212-989-1120
171 West 4th St. *	(6th/7th)	212-675-2303
176 Spring St.	(Thompson/W. Bway)	212-219-8210

THE ORIGINAL LEVI'S STORE

750 Lexington Ave. *	(@ 60th)	212-826-5957
3 East 57th St. *	(5th/Madison)	212-838-2188

TIBET ARTS & CRAFTS

197 Bleecker St. *	(6th/MacDougal)	212-260-5880
144 Sullivan St. *	(Houston/Prince)	212-529-4344

URBAN OUTFITTERS

127 East 59th	(Park/Lex)	212-688-1200
374 Sixth Ave.	(Washington/Waverly)	212-677-9350
628 Broadway*	(Houston/Bleecker)	212-475-0009
162 Second Ave.	(10th/11th)	212-375-1277

VARDA

2080 Broadway	(71st/72nd)	212-873-6910
786 Madison Ave. *	(66th/67th)	212-472-7552
149 Spring St.	(W. B'way/Wooster)	212-941-4990
118 Spring St.	(Green/Mercer)	212-343-9575

VERSACE

815 Madison Ave. *	(68th/69th)	212-744-6868
647 Fifth Ave. *	(@ 52nd)	212-317-0224

VIA SPIGA

765 Madison Ave. *	(65th/66th)	212-988-4877
390 West Broadway*	(Spring/Broome)	212-431-7007

VICTORIA'S SECRET

1240 Third Ave.	(71st/72nd)	212 717-7035
34 E. 57th St. *	(Mad/Park)	212 758-5592
115 Fifth Ave.	(18th/19th)	212 477-4118
565 Broadway	(@ Prince)	212 274-9519
19 Fulton St.	(So St. Seaport)	212 962-8122

UNITED COLORS OF BENETTON

805 Lexington Ave.	(62nd/63rd)	212-752-5283
597 Fifth Ave. *	(48th/49th)	212-317-2501
749 Broadway	(Astor/8th)	212-533-0230

VILLAGE TANNERY

742 Broadway*	(4th/Astor)	212-979-0013
173 Bleecker St. *	(MacDougal/Sullivan)	212-673-5444

ZARA

750 Lexington Ave.	(59th/60th)	212-754-1120
39 West 34th St.	(5th/6th)	212-868-6551
101 Fifth Ave. *	(17th/18th)	212-741-0555
580 Broadway	(Houston/Prince)	212-343-1725

WHERE TO FIND . . . INDEX

COATS

CAR COATS

CLASSIC

CUSTOM

DISCOUNT DESIGNER

UNUSUAL

DRESSES, FORMAL

BEADED

BRIDESMAIDS

CHINESE

CINDERELLA TIL MIDNIGHT/ COUTURE RENTALS

CUSTOM

ECCENTRIC

GLAMOROUS GRAND- MOTHERS

GEN-X

HIP MOMS

SWEATERS

T-SHIRTS

SPECIAL ATTRACTIONS INDEX

STAND-OUT SPACES

ÜBER URBAN

WEARABLE ART

MASTER STORE INDEX

NOTES

ORDER FORM/GIFT FORM

TELEPHONE ORDERS: **888-844-9133**
E-MAIL ORDERS: **orders@fyifashion.com**
ON-LINE ORDERS: **www.fyifashion.com**
MAIL ORDERS: **F.Y.I. Fashion**
                     230 Central Park South
                     Suite 1A
                     New York, NY 10019

Please send _____ (#) copies of **FYI Fashion Source: New York 2000** (ISBN 1-930404-00-X)

PRICE: $14.95 per book

SALES TAX:
Please add 8.25% for products shipped within New York State

SHIPPING:
US: $4 for the 1st book and $2 for each additional.
International: $9 for the 1st book and $5 for each additional.

DISCOUNTS ON BULK ORDERS ARE AVAILABLE.

PAYMENT:
☐ Check   ☐ Mastercard
☐ Visa   ☐ Discover
☐ AMEX

CARD NUMBER _____

NAME ON CARD: _____

EXP. DATE: _____ / _____

NAME (FROM): _____

ADDRESS: _____

CITY: _____

STATE: _____ ZIP: _____ TELEPHONE: _____

E-MAIL: _____

GIFTED TO: _____

ADDRESS: _____

CITY: _____

STATE: _____ ZIP: _____ TELEPHONE: _____